Kings
of Crypto

Kings
_of_ Crypto

**One Startup's Quest _to_
Take Cryptocurrency _out of_
Silicon Valley _and onto_ Wall Street**

JEFF JOHN ROBERTS

Harvard Business Review Press
Boston, Massachusetts

Library of Congress Cataloging-in-Publication Data

Names: Roberts, Jeff John, author.
Title: Kings of crypto : one startup's quest to take cryptocurrency out of
    Silicon Valley and onto Wall Street / Jeff John Roberts.
Description: Boston, MA : Harvard Business Review Press, [2020]
    | Includes index.
Identifiers: LCCN 2020036284 (print) | LCCN 2020036285 (ebook)
    | ISBN 9781647820183 (hardcover) | ISBN 9781647820190 (ebook)
Subjects: LCSH: Armstrong, Brian, 1983- | Cryptocurrencies.
    | Cryptocurrencies–United States. | Money–United States. | Currency question.
Classification: LCC HG1710.3 .R85 2020 (print) | LCC HG1710.3 (ebook)
    | DDC 332.4–dc23
LC record available at https://lccn.loc.gov/2020036284
LC ebook record available at https://lccn.loc.gov/2020036285

ISBN: 978-1-64782-018-3
eISBN: 978-1-64782-019-0

For my wife, Amy

Contents

PART THREE

From Crypto Winter to the Crypto Future

A Note on Sources

I first encountered bitcoin and Coinbase in 2013. I was a reporter at the tech blog *GigaOm*, where I reported on collisions between law and technology—including the then-novel phenomenon of *cryptocurrency*. On a hot July day, I set out to investigate an event called Satoshi Square, which took place in a corner of New York's Union Square. Believing I would need a bitcoin to participate, I bought one for $70 from Coinbase, intending to expense it. Happily, I forgot to do so and ended up holding on to it—and sold half of it later that year when the price hit what seemed to be an absurd high of $800.

Since then, I have been fascinated with cryptocurrency and the role Coinbase has played in bringing it to the general public. I have written about the company numerous times since 2013 for *GigaOm* and for *Fortune* magazine.

In researching this book, I drew on my earlier work and also conducted numerous additional interviews with Coinbase executives and board members. I also interviewed many other influential figures in the cryptocurrency world, including academics, investors, and those close to Coinbase's competitors. Most of the accounts in this book, including nearly all of the quotes attributed to people at Coinbase, are from those interviews.

I have also drawn extensively on secondary material, including news reports from *Wired*, the *New York Times*, *Forbes*, and *Coindesk*. The reporting in *Kings of Crypto* also makes use of the excellent first generation of cryptocurrency histories, including *Digital Gold*, *The Age of Cryptocurrency*, and *Blockchain Revolution*. When I have relied on material directly from these sources for my own narrative, I've made every effort to identify them accordingly.

Finally, this work represents a more polished version of the audio version of *Kings of Crypto*, which came out in May 2020. The book you now hold in your hands includes more recent news surrounding Coinbase and corrects several minor errors.

PART ONE

From Open Secret to Civil War

1

Brian Has
a Secret

Brian Armstrong stepped out of his car, felt soft California
sunshine on his bald head, and smelled eucalyptus. He gazed
at the façade of Y Combinator: the one-story building, just
five miles from Google's Mountain View campus, looked more like
a sleepy suburban office park than a famous startup school that had
educated the founders of Stripe, Dropbox, and other billion-dollar
companies. Brian didn't care about the place's humdrum appearance.
He knew who had gone there before him. The founders of Airbnb, a
company he'd just left, had come out of Y Combinator, and so had the
CEOs of other Silicon Valley stars like Doordash, Twitch, and Reddit.
Brian, pale and shy-looking at first glance, exuded a quiet confidence
from his trim frame and wasn't bothered that he'd broken up with his
would-be cofounder just days before, making him the rare entrepreneur to do the program alone. It was the summer of 2012, and Brian
was brimming with certainty that he would build Y Combinator's
next famous startup.

It wasn't always this way. Twelve miles to the south, in San Jose, is where Brian had spent his early teenage years in the 1990s, restless and vaguely unhappy. San Jose is the tenth-largest city in the country and the hub of Silicon Valley, but it could still feel—then and now—like a lifeless parking lot where many people have nothing to do. Brian felt like that a lot. Until the internet.

As it had for so many other intelligent but introverted kids, the appearance of the World Wide Web brought friends to Brian as well as a flood of exciting ideas. Being stuck in poky San Jose didn't matter now that he had a global community of hackers and philosophers at his keyboard. By the time he arrived at Rice University in 2001, Brian knew he wanted to use the internet to remake the world in the way an earlier generation of tech visionaries had done with microchips and desktop computers.

But there was a problem.

"I always had this thought, 'I wish I was born a bit sooner.' By the time I graduated from college and I was starting to work, I worried maybe I was too late," Brian recalls. "The formative internet companies had been built, and the revolution had happened."

He was wrong, of course. The internet revolution is still blazing, and entrepreneurs, for better and worse, are using it to remake our homes and our lives. And in late 2008, a mysterious person using the name Satoshi Nakamoto published a nine-page white paper on the web that would bring that same revolution to money. Brian discovered that paper a year later.

It was Christmas, and Brian was in his old room back at his parents' house in San Jose, reading tech news on the internet, as usual. Someone had posted Satoshi's paper on a computer discussion forum. Right away, he was rapt. He read and then reread what the paper described: a new type of digital currency known as bitcoin that operated outside the realm of any bank, company, or government. Bitcoin kept track of who paid whom just as a bank did, but the transactions were recorded by random people on computers scattered around the globe. It was real money without banks or borders. Brian began reading Satoshi's paper a third time, ignoring his mother's calls from downstairs to join the family for dinner.

Two and a half years later, as he walked through the doors of Y Combinator, Brian was more fixated on bitcoin than ever. By now, he had developed a special insight of his own about the currency, one that he would soon deliver to millions of people.

. . .

In his startup bible, *Zero to One*, mercurial billionaire Peter Thiel talks about "open secrets"—business ideas that are just there for the plucking by those who are not afraid to challenge conventional thinking. Thiel gives the example of Airbnb, whose founders saw a latent market for empty rooms, and Uber, whose founders realized it was possible to replace taxis with a GPS signal and a smartphone app.

The books of business writer Michael Lewis provide other examples of open secrets. In *Moneyball*, Lewis describes a general manager who built a winning baseball team by relying on data rather than the long-held wisdom of veteran scouts. And in *Liar's Poker*, he recounts how a trader made a killing at his Wall Street firm by bundling home loans into mortgage bonds—an obvious idea, but a secret at the time because popular consensus dismissed it.

In 2012, Brian had grabbed an open secret of his own. He knew bitcoin could be a world-changing technology, but that buying it— for most people—was a confusing, convoluted experience. What if he could make it simpler? Y Combinator President Sam Altman understood the power of such simplicity and what Brian sought to do. "Making things easy to use is important to 99 percent of people, but technical people overlook that. When Dropbox launched, programmers would say, 'I don't get why anyone needs this when you can use these command line tools and make backups of all your files,'" he says, describing a computer process obvious to programmers but baffling to everyone else.

The same reasoning applied to bitcoin. More people would try it if only someone built a website where they could buy it the same way they bought stocks online. But the bitcoin devotees who could build such a site scoffed at the idea. They didn't see the point. Instead, many sought to lift the technical principles of Satoshi's paper and build a cryptocurrency of their own in hopes of getting rich. In Altman's words, "Everyone in the crypto community wanted to start a new version of bitcoin. There was this mindset at the time of, 'I'm going to get rich quick by making a new coin and keeping 20 percent for myself.'"

Brian saw it differently. Seizing on that open secret—the pent-up demand for easy access to bitcoin—he built a mockup of what would become the website Coinbase. And on August 21, 2012, Brian took the stage on Y Combinator's Demo Day, a semiannual event where so many startups strut their stuff before venture capitalists and the tech press. It is a small moment of glory for the founders to savor before, inevitably, most flame out in the following months. That's the ordinary fate of startups, but not all of them, including two other companies in Brian's class: one was Instacart—now a billion-dollar grocery service—and the other Soylent, a meal-replacement product that's since built a cult following in Silicon Valley and beyond.

When it was his turn to present on Demo Day, Brian stepped onto the stage with quiet confidence. He turned to the audience and shared his idea with the simple slogan: "Coinbase: The easiest way to get started with bitcoin."

It seemed so obvious—in retrospect.

. . .

Brian's early insight into bitcoin would make him a billionaire. But it would cost him a friend. In that summer of 2012, Brian had not planned on going to Y Combinator alone, where one-man bands were discouraged. The startup school wanted cofounders. Plural.

Despite Silicon Valley's veneration of individual entrepreneurs, the reality is that tech startups, like so many creative endeavors, are very much a team sport—often a two-person partnership. In works like *Collaborative Circles* and *Powers of Two*, researchers have shown how genius is rarely solitary: John Lennon and Paul McCartney relied on each other to compose timeless Beatles hits; Pablo Picasso and Georges Braque used their brushes side by side to create Cubism; biologists James Watson and Francis Crick worked intensely together to discover the double helix and DNA.

Tech is no different. Apple is famously associated with Steve Jobs, but, in its early days, the computer company wouldn't have gotten off the ground without the other Steve—Jobs's partner and programming virtuoso Steve Wozniak. The same is true with Google. The Stanford graduate supervisor of Larry Page and Sergey Brin has remarked on the near total mind-meld of the search engine founders. And a garage in Palo Alto, known as the birthplace of Silicon Valley and now an official California state landmark, did not belong to a lone inventor but to two men: Bill Hewlett and Dave Packard, who founded HP.

Experience had taught Y Combinator's overseers that a good cofounder is as important as a good business plan. "If you look at the history of successful companies, they've been founded by partners," says Y Combinator's Altman. "In our experience, it's very, very hard to be a single founder. The ups and downs of a startup are so intense that you need to cheer each other up when someone is struggling."

And right up until the start of the Y Combinator program, Brian had a cofounder. His name was Ben Reeves. A shy, young British kid, Ben was a programming wizard who believed in bitcoin with the same passion as Brian. The pair clicked upon meeting on a bitcoin discussion website. Before long, Brian and Ben made plans to start a company together. They applied to Y Combinator as a team, and the prestigious school accepted them. But days before Ben was due to board a plane from the UK, the pair clashed on a key issue and Brian jilted him. "Cofounding is really like a marriage. Even though I think we have mutual respect for each other, we don't work together extremely well," Brian emailed Ben a few days before Y Combinator.

For good measure, Brian changed the passwords to the libraries of code they had been building together. In startup land, it was the equivalent of cutting off a spouse from a joint bank account. But it had to be done.

The point on which Brian and Ben had disagreed wasn't an aesthetic one or even a strategic one. It was an existential one. Their dispute turned on a near-religious clash about what bitcoin was supposed to be.

When the pseudonymous Satoshi Nakamoto revealed bitcoin in his nine-page paper, he described the invention of a new and decentralized technology. That word, *decentralized*, is critical. It meant no single person, company, or government could control the network on which bitcoin is built. Meanwhile, people who bought and sold bitcoin could not rely on a bank or anyone else to manage their stash of digital money. Owning bitcoin meant using something called a *private key*—a long gobbledygook string of letters, numbers, and symbols—that opened and closed your online wallet. If a person lost that key, it was gone forever. It was the digital equivalent of a pile of cash in an unbreakable safe to which no one knew the combination.

That's where Coinbase came in. Brian's idea—the open secret he seized on—was to provide a service where you could own bitcoin without controlling a private key. Coinbase would do it for you.

It was a commonsense solution. But bitcoin purists saw it as heresy, against everything Satoshi stood for. It didn't matter that customers could use Coinbase to buy bitcoin and then transfer it to a wallet they controlled with a private key. It was a matter of principle. In the eyes of the purists—the overwhelming majority in the crypto community back in 2012—Brian and his vision of Coinbase stood for the c-word: *centralization*. He was a heretic and a traitor to Satoshi's vision.

Brian and Ben never reconciled. Ben would go on to build a successful bitcoin company of his own, but he has never forgotten how Brian had jilted him. Years later, he allowed *Wired* magazine to publish verbatim the text of Brian's break-up email. His LinkedIn page still reads, "Coinbase founding team member."

Brian today plays down the rift. The divorce with Ben came at the prodding of a senior executive at Y Combinator, and Brian believes it was necessary. But at the time, it was also a major problem. As a result of his last-minute breakup with Ben, Brian became the rare entrepreneur to go through Y Combinator as a single founder. In doing so, he had reaped the accelerator's coaching experience and could tap into its fantastic Rolodex of mentors and investors. But he had no one to cheer him up or encourage him when things got hard. And they were about to get very hard.

While Y Combinator offered prestige and publicity because of the small number of companies it accepted into its fold, acceptance was not the same as success. The reality was, after the program's much-hyped Demo Day, over 80 percent of the startups quietly ran out of money and turned to dust. And those companies typically had two or three founders pulling out all the stops. In the summer of 2012, Coinbase was little more than a marketing idea and an unfinished website with a single founder. The company needed much more to get off the ground—millions more lines of code, product testing, a business plan and, of course, real-life customers. If Brian couldn't pull this off, Coinbase would share the fate of most startups: failure. Brian's odds were grim.

· · ·

Five miles south of Y Combinator in Mountain View is another Silicon Valley town called Sunnyvale. It has the same soft air, eucalyptus scent, bland suburban streets, and a stop for the Cal-Train, the region's poky commuter rail service. It's home to dozens of notable tech companies, including Atari, Yahoo, Palm, and the chip maker AMD. That same summer of 2012, it also become home to a young Wall Street refugee named Fred Ehrsam.

Fred was one of those golden kids everyone knows in high school. He had a model's good looks—a chiseled face and a flop of blond hair—and he radiated swashbuckling athleticism. Growing up in Concord, New Hampshire, he had run with the popular crowd—of course he did—but it never felt right.

"I felt like an observer of my own life," he says. He did what he was supposed to do: got good grades, excelled at lacrosse and basketball. The desire to please his father gnawed at him. Fred's dad was a hard-charging engineer who had graduated from Harvard Business School and expected the world. Years later, staring out from a magnificent penthouse with bountiful views of the city of San Francisco and the ocean beyond, Fred still didn't know if he measured up. "Even if you're very good at a video game, the levels keep getting harder and harder," he said wistfully.

Fred's choice of metaphor is fitting. Video games are something he knows better than almost anyone else. Although the world around him in high school never felt right, the one he found on the internet sure did. Every day, he would leave lacrosse or basketball practice as soon as he could and rush to play *World of Warcraft* or *Call of Duty*, often staying up all night so he could stay competitive in two online leagues—one in the US and another in Europe. By the time he was a senior, he was a professional gamer, entering and winning tournaments around the country.

Video games gave Fred an escape from the pressures of high school and family life, but only a temporary one. Soon enough, it would be time to get a college degree, which he earned as a computer science student at Duke University, and then it was time to make a respectable living. And he did, taking a job as a foreign exchange trader at Goldman Sachs. "Being a forex trader at Goldman Sachs was the closest I could get to playing a video game in real life while also having a job that came with money and prestige," he admits.

Fred looked the part, and he was good at the job. That didn't mean he liked it. In fact, he was dying inside. His bosses at Goldman Sachs were old-school Wall Street types who had come up bellowing into telephones and jostling with other men in trading pits. And they didn't like the new style of trading that was creeping into the finance industry, one that largely rewarded those who wrote the best algorithms. The prophecy of the famous West Coast venture capitalist (and future Coinbase board member) Marc Andreessen, "Software is eating the world," was coming true. And it was going to swallow up those old-school traders. Even if they didn't want to admit it.

"They called the software engineers 'IT' and treated them as second class," Fred recalls. "They had this aversion to automation. If I wanted to do something that could replace half the trading desk, they didn't want that. It was a very bizarre time."

It was like high school all over again. On the surface, Fred looked and acted the part of a hotshot trader, and he was pleasing his parents, but deep inside he wished he was anywhere else. So he responded as he had back then, taking refuge late at night on the internet, discovering people and worlds and a place he belonged. This time, he became transfixed by blogs and Reddit threads about a new digital currency that anyone could access without a central bank—or, for that matter, a merchant bank like Goldman Sachs. Bitcoin, a currency free of governments, wasn't just an intriguing idea, Fred felt. It was a necessary one. Day after day, he watched Wall Street gorge itself on Federal Reserve funds. The situation overseas was even worse—countries like Greece fumbled from bailout to bailout as a result of epic mismanagement by political leaders. In contrast, the once-crazy concept of bitcoin looked sane. Also, Fred saw in bitcoin a job for which he was born: he knew about digital money from years of using video game currency, and he knew about finance as a Wall Street trader. He wanted in on bitcoin.

There was just one problem. All of the action appeared to be taking place in Silicon Valley. This was a place he'd heard about, of course, but growing up in New England, he didn't grok what it was all about. Gradually, though, he came to realize—just as painters flocked to Paris and moviemakers to Hollywood—Silicon Valley was where you went if you wanted to do great things with software. Even New York City, which supposedly had everything, didn't offer that particular mix of business hustle and computer science wizardry. It was time to go. After two years at Goldman, Fred took leave of the tall buildings of Wall Street and struck out for suburban Sunnyvale.

. . .

Fred and Brian met at The Creamery. Like so many other famous Silicon Valley venues, The Creamery doesn't look like much: a low-slung, single-story wooden building with white letters above the doorframe; a small patio; some seat-yourself indoor tables; a menu of breakfast sandwiches, salads, and the usual assortment of cocktails and cappuccinos. It's a modest place on a nondescript San Francisco street corner, yet its walls have heard billions of dollars' worth of venture capital deals and countless startup pitches for massive successes and failures alike.

Maybe The Creamery is popular because it's right near a freeway off-ramp and a Cal-Train station. Maybe it's because patrons can walk right in and out, with no fuss. Or maybe it's just because tech people have always met there. (Its numerous well-heeled customers could not help The Creamery survive the pandemic, however. The famous establishment closed in August of 2020.)

In Brian's case, he chose The Creamery because it was right across the street from the makeshift office he had rented at 1 Bluxome Street. He had wrapped up at Y Combinator a few months before with a bulging list of contacts and potential investors, while the startup school—as it does with everyone who enrolls—took 7 percent of his company. Still, Brian was very much alone, professionally and personally, when Fred replied to one of his bitcoin threads on Reddit.

Fred had left Sunnyvale a few weeks before, where he had been bunking with old college friends, and was now living in San Francisco. When he met Brian, it was like one of those rare Tinder dates that actually clicks. "Something felt right in my gut about this. It just felt exciting," Fred recalls. This emerging company called Coinbase felt like a rollicking video game he had never played before. But it was real.

The bromance between the mid-twenty-somethings was mutual. If Brian had had cold feet about a startup marriage with Ben, this time he was ready to jump in quickly. In Fred, he had found a cofounder, a friend, and a fellow fanatic. Together, they bashed their keyboards around the clock, often working sixteen-hour days as they struggled to compile the code that would let people do what hadn't been done before: acquire bitcoin simply by providing a bank account number. No overseas wire transfers, no intimidating mathematical strings— just a basic website that felt like online banking.

It had been nearly four months since Brian had taken the stage at Y Combinator. Now, in November of 2012, it was time to see if Coinbase was for real. It was time to launch a feature to buy and sell bitcoin with one click. A whisper of San Francisco fog sat outside the window as Brian and Fred huddled anxiously over a laptop as the feature went live.

· · ·

Success!

A trickle of customer orders came dribbling into the website. Weeks later, it was a stampede. Word got around about this new and easy way to buy bitcoin. Volume increased, and so did their workload as Brian and Fred struggled to keep the site up and running.

The first crisis came when a software bug skewed the appearance of customers' bitcoin balance. On the Coinbase side, things were fine— the bitcoin was there—but for some customers, it looked like they had been wiped out. Coinbase's crude customer service portal flashed with dozens, then hundreds, then more than two thousand frantic requests from panicked clients.

"Where the hell is my bitcoin?" "Is this a scam?" "Give me my money back!" The anxious, often abusive, invective kept pouring in. It was a critical moment for a fragile startup with an even more fragile reputation in an industry fraught with distrust. Brian and Fred worked around the clock, taking turns sleeping on the floor while the other beat back the cascade of customer requests and repaired the bug.

Finally, following hour after hour of exhaustive coding, the fire was out and the site was fixed. Coinbase's credibility was restored. Brian, calm as ever, turned back to reading tech news. Fred, too frugal to take an Uber, stumbled toward home in San Francisco's notorious Tenderloin district, whose streets jangled with broken glass and the screams of junkies. Fred passed through it all oblivious. At one point, he shuffled for two blocks behind a blind man who staggered pitifully down the wretched sidewalks.

Finally, Fred found his way into his bed. People outside were still stirring.

2

The Outlaw Currency

Katie Haun typed the letters F-N-U L-N-U on the new criminal file—"first name unknown, last name unknown." It's how federal prosecutors refer to suspects yet to be identified. They pronounce it "fe-new el-new."

Haun was glad for the opportunity to track down this FNU LNU, whomever he was.

A blonde woman brimming with energy, she had arrived in San Francisco in 2009 as someone streaking to the top of the legal world. Haun had clerked for Justice Anthony Kennedy at the Supreme Court—a ticket to whatever high-paying job she liked. Instead, she had chosen to work for the feds. For three years now, her job had revolved around some of the most violent degenerates in the Northern District of California, and she prosecuted them with zeal: organized crime bosses, biker gangs that brutally murdered their rivals. She put them on trial and sent them to prison. The work was interesting as hell, but she was ready for something new, something less bloody.

This FNU LNU character fit the bill. Details were sketchy—all her superiors could tell her was that the case involved computers and a whole lot of illegal activity. "My boss came in and said, 'How would you like to prosecute this other new thing called bitcoin?' I had never heard about it at the time," Haun recalls.

Still, she said yes immediately.

• • •

The idea of prosecuting a currency seems ridiculous. It makes as much sense to put bitcoin on trial as it does to cross-examine a hundred-dollar bill. But for prosecutors in 2012, unclear on what bitcoin was but clear on what was happening around it, it made sense. The digital money kept turning up in a whole spate of criminal activity—from money laundering to drug sales to extortion. Many in law enforcement were connecting dots between the currency and crimes. Some kingpin surely had a hand in all of this.

It didn't take Haun long, though, to figure out that her FNU LNU suspect was not a crime boss or mob outfit. It was a radical new technology. And so she did what most people do when they become interested in bitcoin. She started reading.

Bitcoin newcomers quickly discover the subject is a rabbit hole, and that it can take hundreds of hours to learn the ins and outs of topics like "hash rate" and "consensus mechanism." Haun didn't need to know all that. She needed to know the basics. And at the most basic level, she realized that bitcoin is a computer program, albeit a very clever one. Anyone can download and run it on a home laptop. On its own like that, it's not that inspiring, or even useful. The cleverness—the magic of bitcoin—is that it runs on thousands of computers around the world. And together, all of those computers are creating a permanent ledger of transactions that show who's spending the digital money the program creates. Collectively, they're a bookkeeper that never takes a break and holds a record of every bitcoin transaction ever made. A bitcoin spent in 2010 appears on the ledger for all to see today. A millionth of a bitcoin paid today—yes, that's possible—will show up on the ledger within minutes and never leave it. It can't be removed or erased, and everyone can see it. Bitcoin also uses fancy math to make every transaction nonrepudiable; that is, both technically and legally, there's no disputing that it happened.

The transactions don't appear one at a time. Instead, every ten minutes or so, one of the computers on the network rounds up a new series of the most recent transactions and stuffs them into a package of computer code called a *block*. Each new block refers to the one that came before it, resulting in a long series of transactions wrapped into parcels and visible to everyone. It's called the *blockchain*. Today, there are many blockchains, and the term can refer to any piece of software that relies on multiple computers to create a ledger of transactions. But the bitcoin blockchain is the first and the most famous one.

The first block appeared on the bitcoin blockchain in 2009 when bitcoin's shadowy creator, Satoshi Nakamoto, put it there. Since then, computers around the world have added more than half a million additional blocks. At the end of 2019, block 600,000 arrived. It was chained to block 599,999 and, like the others before it, it contained a list of transactions showing how people spent bitcoin. The blockchain doesn't spell out the names of who owns each stash of bitcoin. Instead, it shows a long jumble of letters and numbers associated with each bitcoin owner. Everyone on the blockchain has one of these number-letter jumbles. They're called *addresses*. If this sounds familiar, that's because this concept of a jumble of letters and numbers came up earlier in the context of a private key, which is how an owner gets access to the bitcoin associated with a given address. The important thing to know is the computer program assigns every bitcoin owner *two* number-letter jumbles: one for the address everyone sees on the ledger and the other for the private key needed to access their bitcoin.

What Brian did by creating Coinbase was remove all the complexity around addresses and private keys in the first place and let people get bitcoin in a way that resembled online banking. Storing private keys on thumb drives and special software wallets was well and good for techies. Most other people, though, couldn't be bothered. They preferred to turn to a technical middleman: Coinbase.

Coinbase, however, still uses the blockchain. When it buys and sells bitcoin on behalf of its customers, it generates transactions packaged into blocks and added to the ever-growing ledger, just like any other. But unless you knew which address Coinbase was using for a transaction, you would be hard-pressed to know the company was involved. That's the thing about bitcoin: even though the blockchain is public for everyone to see, you don't know to whom a given stash of bitcoin belongs unless the owner identifies the address as their own. The blockchain might show $1 million worth of bitcoin sitting in an address that could belong to a Silicon Valley big shot or a Russian oligarch or some college kid in Korea. Today, a number of blockchain forensics firms can, in some cases, make a good guess about who controls a given bitcoin address itself. But in many other cases—especially when the owners of accounts are careful about covering their tracks—there's no way to know whose transaction is showing up on the ledger. This is the brilliance, and some say the danger, of bitcoin as a truly anonymous currency. It's also why Katie Haun and other members of law enforcement thought bitcoin could only be the creation of a secret criminal mastermind.

But for all bitcoin's technical elegance and brilliance, there's still one more bit of engineering—this time social—required to make bitcoin go. The blockchain ledger requires a distributed network of volunteer computers. Why would anyone go to the trouble of lending their computer to this global record-keeping system? Satoshi thought of this incentive problem, too. His answer was an ingenious lottery system baked into the core of bitcoin. This system invites anyone to enter a contest to win bitcoin by solving a math problem that can only be deduced through a massive process of trial and error. The contest takes place every ten minutes or so, and whoever is first to find the answer broadcasts it to the other computers on the network. In doing so, that person adds the latest block—which contains both the solution to the math problem and the most recent batch of bitcoin transactions—to the ledger. Provided the solution is correct, the lottery participants—known as *miners* in the bitcoin world—move on to solving the next math problem. For their trouble, winners gets a stash of bitcoin associated with each block. Some people call this stash the *block reward*. Some call it the *coinbase*.

Bitcoin's blockchain and reward system is clever—brilliant, even. But that doesn't explain why bitcoin are worth anything in the first place. After all, bitcoin aren't even coins. They amount to no more than wisps of computer code you can't see or touch.

But that doesn't matter. Bitcoin is currency, and currency is trust. What matters is that enough people agree bitcoin are worth something and will give up something of value to get them. In this sense, bitcoin is no different than any other currency people have used over the course of history: shells, chunks of yellow metal, pieces of paper printed by a bank or government. Right now, tens of millions of people believe bitcoin is valuable—and will pay thousands of dollars to own one coin.

In the beginning, bitcoin was worth what skeptics say it should be worth: nothing. Well, nearly nothing. In early 2010, a handful of online exchanges sprang up selling dozens of bitcoin for mere pennies. These exchanges offered an easier way to get hold of bitcoin than trying to mine them through a math-problem lottery. But for most people at the time, buying bitcoin with US dollars made as much sense as trading a cow for magic beans. It was a make-believe currency for fools and fanatics.

Then, on May 22, 2010, bitcoin gained currency, literally. A Florida man named Laszlo Hanyecz sought to show the world that bitcoin could be worth something in the real world. On an online forum, Laszlo made an offer: "I'll pay 10,000 bitcoin for a couple of pizzas . . . like maybe two large ones so I have some left over for the next day." A fellow in the UK accepted the offer. He received the 10,000 bitcoin—then worth around $35—and sent two Papa John's pies to Laszlo's house. The bitcoin-for-pizza swap made news in tech outlets around the world, and the wave of publicity helped the price pop. If Laszlo had done the transaction a year later, in 2011, his 10,000 bitcoin would have bought him hundreds of pizzas while, a decade letter, he could have used the bitcoin to buy dozens of Papa John's franchises. At the time, though, Laszlo was just trying to make a point—and he did. He has since become a minor celebrity and his purchase is celebrated annually as bitcoin Pizza Day. Nine years after the event, with bitcoin's value having skyrocketed since his pizza buy, Laszlo sat down on CBS's *60 Minutes*, where Anderson Cooper asked what it felt like to have blown his 10,000 bitcoin, which at the time of the interview was worth $80 million, on two pizzas. "I think thinking like this is not really good for me," a stammering Laszlo tells the camera, before adding that he is simply happy to be the hero of bitcoin's official holiday.

By 2012, when Brian started Coinbase, a bitcoin was no longer worth pennies but a few dollars. Now, millions of people around the world knew what it was and how to use it. What people—including Assistant US Attorney Katie Haun and her boss—still did not know was, who was behind it? There was only that nine-page paper by the person with the strange pseudonym: Satoshi Nakamoto.

So who is Satoshi Nakamoto? This is a taboo topic among most bitcoin believers, who don't like to discuss it. This is by design. As authors Paul Vigna and Michael Casey explain in *The Age of Cryptocurrency*, bitcoin is a religion as much as it is a technology. And like every good religion, its origin story is surrounded in sacred mystery. Asking a bitcoin fan to disclose Satoshi's real identity is like asking an observant Jewish person to say the name of the Lord or a Christian to explain the virgin birth. Faith doesn't require explanation.

Be this as it may, there's enough evidence to make a strong guess about who the white paper's author really is. The signs point to an American polymath named Nick Szabo.

Szabo is a lawyer and sophisticated coder with deep ties to an online community, known as *cypherpunks*, that spent years experimenting with digital money. This community shares a love of cryptography and a deep distrust of government, which is reflected in Szabo's Twitter feed and rare public appearances. While there are other cypherpunks closely associated with the first days of bitcoin—notably, the late programmer Hal Finney—some big clues point to Szabo as the paper's author. These include anecdotes, set out by *New York Times* reporter and *Digital Gold* author Nathaniel Popper, that put Szabo at the center of early development of bitcoin. Additionally, linguists have compared the white paper and Satoshi's emails with writing samples from Szabo, Finney, and other possible candidates. Szabo is far and away the closest match. Satoshi Nakamoto's initials are also the inverse of Nick Szabo's. It could be a coincidence. All of it could be a coincidence. But if you subscribe to the philosophical principle known as Occam's Razor, which holds that simpler solutions are more likely to be correct than complex ones, it makes far more sense to accept that Szabo is the author than to insist it's either someone else or a mystery incapable of being unraveled. In fact, most longtime bitcoin owners will concede quietly in a one-on-one conversation that they, too, accept Szabo as Satoshi. Just don't ask them to do it publicly.

Today, it doesn't really matter if Szabo is Satoshi. Bitcoin has evolved past the paper and one person or a small group of people. The currency and its backbone, the blockchain, pulses on thousands of computers around the world, and no army or government could get rid of it, short of turning off the internet.

Even back in 2012, the proverbial toothpaste was out of the tube. When Katie Haun's boss asked her to investigate Mr. FNU LNU, the chance to shut down bitcoin was gone. Maybe two years earlier, when bitcoin first began to circulate, it might have been possible to halt it by rounding up the early users and seizing their computers. Maybe. But that window had long closed. The more Haun learned, the less the notion of filing criminal charges against bitcoin made sense to her.

"It's like you would prosecute cash. It wasn't something you could do," recalls Haun.

She was right. By 2012, bitcoin had given rise to a full-fledged economy. A Papa John's pizza purchase might have been a novelty in 2010, but now a growing number of merchants were accepting bitcoin directly. Some people even aspired to live on bitcoin.

• • •

Olaf Carlson-Wee was a skinny blond kid resembling an elf from *Lord of the Rings*—if elves hung around skate parks. As a teenager, he followed his dreams, literally. He took up a deep interest in the phenomenon of dreaming. He studied neurology to learn what causes dreams and, through practice and by reading authors like Carlos Castaneda, he learned how to turn sleep into profound, vivid quests.

Olaf even claims he learned to wield magical-type powers when he sleeps. "In a lucid dream, find a mirror. If you get good at lucid dreaming, you can summon things using a mirror. If you walk so close to the mirror that you lose peripheral vision, then you can summon yourself," he says.

Face to face with the other Olaf in the mirror, Carlson-Wee says he would pose questions. He had control over the questions but not the answers, which the other Olaf would supply. Those answers—summoned from somewhere deep in his psyche and released in the dream—often scared the hell out of him. It's no surprise that the eight hundred other students in his rural Minnesota high school voted Olaf as "most unique."

Olaf discovered bitcoin in early 2011 and, like other things he cared about, he didn't just like it—he obsessed over it. The child of two Lutheran pastors, Olaf had been raised to live according to his conscience and explore the meaning of justice. Later, during the financial carnage of the Great Recession—where millions of ordinary people, including his parents, had their hard-won savings wiped out while the bank executives most responsible received bonuses—Olaf saw bitcoin as an economic system that could not be rigged.

"This was the ultimate cyberpunk authoritarian thing," he recalls. He plowed almost all of his life savings of $700 into bitcoin and urged his friends to do the same.

In his final year at Vassar College in upstate New York, not long before Brian left Airbnb for Y Combinator and Katie Haun's boss asked her to prosecute FNU LNU, Olaf selected bitcoin as the topic for his final thesis. His professor was bemused at first, then tried to discourage Olaf after discovering "The Rise and Fall of Bitcoin," an article that appeared in the November 2011 edition of *Wired* magazine. The article concluded that the upstart currency was a failure based on a market meltdown that saw the price fall from $31 to $2.

"Pick another topic," said the professor. Olaf, a full-fledged bitcoin believer, refused. He doubled down on his research and made a sweeping economic case for why digital currency would change the world. The professor gave him an A+. (It probably didn't hurt that, by the time Olaf submitted his thesis in 2012, the price of bitcoin had inched back up to $10.)

During all this time, Olaf kept buying bitcoin. This was no easy task in Poughkeepsie, New York, population 30,000. Sometimes it meant meeting someone on campus who would sell bitcoin for cash. Often, Olaf had to resort to more exotic measures such as placing a deposit into the account of some shadowy online money transfer operation. This entailed walking into a local bank and depositing a very specific amount—say $103.83—that served as a code to tell the operators which bitcoin address belonged to Olaf. If all went smoothly, the corresponding amount of bitcoin would show up in Olaf's account, minus a stiff transaction fee. If it didn't go smoothly, Olaf would get burned—receiving no bitcoin for the money. Maybe the site he paid had been hacked and all the bitcoin were gone or, just as likely, the site owners had pulled an exit scam—claiming they had been hacked and then vanishing into the ether of the internet with his cash.

"Those were scrappy times," Olaf recalls. "Getting bitcoin was a hard thing. Those days, everything got hacked, everything was an exit scam. There was a site called 'Mybitcoin' to buy from, and the joke was it had that name because the site owners treated it as 'my bitcoin, not yours.'"

When Coinbase came on the scene, it was a godsend for a bitcoin believer like Olaf. Finally, here was a site that promised to make bitcoin easy to get—and was trying hard not to be shady. The company was based in California, not overseas, and you could see who was running it: a guy named Brian Armstrong, whom you could Google, and who talked about things like compliance and regulation. Those were dirty words to the antigovernment zealots who had helped bitcoin gain traction in the first place, but they sounded great to Olaf. Like Brian, he thought the only way his beloved currency would catch on in the mainstream was if ordinary people could get it and not get scammed.

"You heard the same taunts a lot about Coinbase—'not your keys, not your coins,'" Olaf says. That phrase popped up on Reddit threads about bitcoin and reminded people that they were trusting a company to manage their stash of digital gold. A heresy in the church of Satoshi.

And so it was that even though Coinbase introduced cryptocurrency to millions of non-technical people, many of bitcoin's early champions reviled the company. These included the radical libertarian Erik Voorhees, who had denounced the Federal Reserve as "fraudulent," and Roger Ver, a flamboyant figure known as "Bitcoin Jesus" for his habit of giving away bitcoin while proselytizing about the currency. In 2014, Ver renounced his American citizenship over a professed belief in open borders. (That was his explanation at least—skeptics think it was tax avoidance more than principles that motivated Ver.) Whatever their true intentions, figures like Voorhees and Ver were the public faces of bitcoin in the early days, believers who inspired others to adopt the currency, and a worldview that saw Coinbase as a betrayal of Satoshi's vision.

Some people saw Voorhees and Ver as saints. Olaf just thought they were nuts. Coinbase, he reasoned, didn't betray bitcoin—it gave people a way to get it. Once they did, they could transfer their crypto treasure to their own software wallet, a hard drive, or a USB drive. It was up to them. For people with ordinary tech savvy, the difference between Coinbase and managing their own bitcoin was like the difference between learning to drive an automatic Toyota Corolla compared with a stick-shift eighteen-wheeler with ten speeds and two reverse speeds. A Corolla might be boring, but anyone could drive it.

Olaf adopted Coinbase and also wanted Coinbase to adopt him. He wanted to join the company. And that was a problem, since he'd never applied for a real job before. After college, he had gone full bohemian—spending months tramping around the Sierra Nevada mountains in California before finally landing a gig as a lumberjack in an outpost called Holden Village in Washington State. Holden Village had been a deserted copper mining town remade as a Lutheran revival center by hippies in the 1960s, and it offered three square meals and a yurt to sleep in for those willing to work there. It suited Olaf just fine, save the fact it was far away—figuratively and literally—from bitcoin.

Despite his lack of a resume or any other obvious qualifications, Olaf applied for a job. He emailed Fred Ehrsam and attached his thesis. He mentioned his A+ grade. Fred wrote back right away. Olaf had his first job interview.

This meant turning up weeks later at Coinbase's office in San Francisco. Olaf had friends in the city who were glad to let him couch-surf, but his clothes were a problem, still covered with sap stains from his lumberjack work. At his friends' urging, Olaf hit a Uniqlo and bought one clean white shirt, tearing off the packaging and donning the new garment right before ringing the buzzer on Bluxome Street across from the Creamery.

At the time, Brian and Fred were asking job candidates to make two fifteen-minute presentations—one on their vision for Coinbase and the other on a topic of their choice to teach the pair something they didn't know. Fred also liked to throw in a logic puzzle, like the ones used in the early days of Google, to test prospective employees' analytic chops.

They posed this to Olaf: "So there are one hundred lockers in a row. They're all closed. A kid goes by and opens every single locker. A second kid goes by and closes every other locker. A third kid comes by and, for every third locker, he opens it if it's closed and closes it if it's open. Same deal for the fourth kid, who changes the state of every fourth locker. A hundred kids go by. How many lockers are open?"

Oh shit, thought Olaf. Fred had given him a few minutes to figure it out, but Olaf knew it would take him much, much longer to run through the sequence. There had to be a trick. Olaf, a sociology major, also liked math, and he realized the locker problem was about perfect squares—the answer would be obvious for numbers like 25 or 64 or . . . 100 lockers. He told Fred the answer: 10 lockers. One hurdle passed.

For his presentations, Olaf sketched out a plan to fix the dumpster fire of a public relations situation at Coinbase because Brian and Fred couldn't keep up with the volume of business. They liked his plan. For his teach-us-something-we-don't-know presentation, Olaf tapped into his favorite topic after bitcoin: dreams. He explained how ingesting certain over-the-counter drugs like valerian could induce especially lucid dreams, adding details from all the neurology books he had read. They found the dream presentation weird, but interesting. And Brian and Fred learned something.

Olaf had been Coinbase customer number thirty. Now he was hire number one. The drifter-lumberjack now had an office job, and his friends told him that meant he had to look the part. Olaf turned up the next day and every day for the next two weeks in his one white Uniqlo shirt.

In San Francisco, Olaf found a growing community of other bitcoin believers, merchants who had started to accept bitcoin as payment.

He was far from Holden Village now. To his delight, he discovered he could pay for meals, drinks, and other day-to-day essentials with his magic money. And whatever he couldn't buy with bitcoin in the city of San Francisco, he could obtain online from crypto-friendly websites. Soon, Olaf decided that not only *could* he live on bitcoin, he *would* live on bitcoin. For the next three years, that's what he did.

• • •

It wasn't just in San Francisco that bitcoin was breaking through. In cities across the United States—and in places like Prague, Tokyo, and Adelaide, Australia—people were coming together for "bitcoin meet-ups" where they talked about a world beyond the control of governments while buying, selling, or sometimes just giving away bitcoin. Every Monday in New York City, a corner of Union Square turned into "Satoshi Square." It was a strange sight. Crypto-anarchists with dreadlocks mingled with Wall Street traders wearing $5,000 suits and clutching fat stacks of bills, all of them gone mad for bitcoin. The open-air trading space harked back to one more than two hundred years earlier, when popular lore says men in Manhattan first traded stocks under a buttonwood tree.

Many of the people at the meetups were like Olaf, using bitcoin for fun or in the name of some ideal. Unfortunately for the credibility of the young currency, they were far from the only ones using bitcoin. So were drug dealers, money launderers, hit men, extortionists, and every sort of hustler and lowlife imaginable. Satoshi's invention, it turned out, was a criminal's dream: an anonymous currency that could be used to pay anyone, anywhere.

The wider world first learned of bitcoin's criminal potential in 2011 when the muckraking website Gawker published a now-famous article titled "The Underground Website Where You Can Buy Any Drug Imaginable." The article described the Silk Road, a multimillion-dollar online crime bazaar run by a shadowy figure called Dread Pirate Roberts. As Nick Bilton explains in his page-turning account of the Silk Road, *American Kingpin*, the Dread Pirate was only able to pull off what he did thanks to the arrival of three new technologies. The first was the web browsing software called Tor, which let people browse "dark web" sites like Silk Road undetected. The second was the proliferation of cheap, new cloud computing services that let anyone run a massive website on the cheap. The third magic ingredient was bitcoin. Until it arrived, there was no quick and easy way for strangers to pay each other for illegal transactions on the internet. Now it was a relative cinch. Little wonder that law enforcement figures like Katie Haun's boss took a dim view of bitcoin and asked her to open an investigation.

Haun soon realized her FNU LNU was not a criminal mastermind, and that bitcoin was not intrinsically bad or good. Bitcoin was like another once-novel technology: paper money. A stack of $100 bills can finance a drug deal or be donated to an orphanage. Bitcoin is no different, despite its perception as an outlaw currency.

Haun found that the more she learned about bitcoin, the more she wanted to know. She talked to special agents from the FBI, the IRS, and the Secret Service, all of whom told her how bitcoin kept turning up in their cases. Some mentioned a company called Coinbase. Haun figured she would pay a visit. It didn't take long for her to see the Coinbase guys fit a stereotype. But these were not mafia wise guys or cop-hating biker gangs she was used to prosecuting. Instead, she saw tech nerds.

"I had a sense they were more like your traditional startup than people trying to run a criminal operation," she says. "Criminals don't welcome you to come by the office."

3

Running through Brick Walls

High above Market Street, Fred and Brian stared at the sun breaking through fog-dappled San Francisco Bay. Coinbase didn't have anything resembling a real boardroom on Bluxome Street, so they had borrowed space at LendingClub, whose posh corporate headquarters would be the backdrop for a make-or-break meeting.

It was April of 2013—less than a year after Brian's Y Combinator stint and just five months since they'd turned Coinbase on—and the startup needed more money. Brian and Fred had put all the pieces in place to persuade venture capitalists to open their cash spigots and crown Coinbase with a Series A round—a multimillion-dollar investment that would let the company ramp up operations and signal to Silicon Valley that rich, influential people believed in Brian's vision. Then Fred saw it. His stomach sank as he watched the team from Union Square Ventures file in, without Fred Wilson.

"We are so fucked," he said to Brian.

Fred Wilson is the mercurial cofounder of Union Square Ventures, one of a handful of New York City–based VC firms that rivals the prestige of the august Silicon Valley outfits. He is scheming, cold-blooded, and brilliant. As a board member at Twitter, Wilson had presided as a cruel puppet master—summarily purging not just one, but two CEOs. His relationship with the press is famously fractious. Upon learning a reporter was contacting his associates after he had refused to cooperate for a magazine profile, Wilson had warned the journalist that he "might want to think about making friends instead of pissing people off."

Wilson is ruthless, yes, but he's also been a mentor to a generation of startup founders. And unlike other venture capitalists, he was an early bitcoin believer. Satoshi Nakamoto's creation, he thought, could change the world—if only someone could act as a cheerleader who was neither a zealot like Roger Ver nor a criminal like those Katie Haun had heard about from her FBI colleagues. In Brian and Fred, he saw a public face for the technology: two buttoned-up young men with entrepreneurial spirits.

Unfortunately, on this particular May morning, Wilson was home sick in New York City. This left Brian and Fred to make their pitch to the other partners at Union Square Ventures, none of whom shared Wilson's enthusiasm.

"We are so fucked," Fred said again.

The words echoed in Brian's head as he played it forward: What would happen if Union Square Ventures failed to pony up? Like other graduates of the Y Combinator program, he had scraped together a series of $50,000 investments to fund Coinbase's seed round—the little pot of money a new company needs to try to get off the ground. Those investors included the cofounder of Reddit, Alexis Ohanian, whose future wife—tennis star Serena Williams—would, years later, also invest in Coinbase. Brian had also persuaded the entrepreneur Barry

Silbert to chip in. Silbert, who had become a stockbroker at the age of seventeen, had been buying masses of bitcoin since 2012, and when his wife insisted he diversify his wealth, he began investing in cryptocurrency companies too.

Upon approaching Coinbase, however, Silbert was taken aback when Brian told him he could buy in but only in the form of an uncapped convertible note. Such an arrangement would give Silbert the right to receive shares in Coinbase's Series A round, but with a big drawback: "uncapped" meant there was no limit to how much Barry's investment could be diluted by competing investors. Typically, only the hottest of hot startups have the clout to demand an uncapped note, and Silbert, who had invested in dozens of companies, had never agreed to such terms.

"If you believe Coinbase has the best shot to be the number-one wallet, the valuation is almost irrelevant. Look at PayPal. The investors are rich, and the investors in number-two got nothing," Brian wrote to Silbert. It was a cocky email, but it also amused and impressed Silbert, persuading him to take a flyer on Coinbase. He decided to invest $100,000—in bitcoin.

These early investments from Ohanian, Silbert, and others got Coinbase up and running, but that's it. If the company wanted to scale—Silicon Valley–speak for growing into a colossus—Brian and Fred needed venture capital firms to rain down millions of dollars. And making it rain cash required Coinbase to show it was moving "up and to the right." For venture capitalists, the phrase is a near-holy invocation. Up and to the right. It means a startup is adding both users and revenue month after month, making a beautiful diagonal line on their PowerPoint slides.

Since late 2012, Coinbase had been up and to the right. On three occasions, Brian and Fred had taken their beautiful line to

Paul Graham, the cofounder of Y Combinator and their rabbi of fundraising. The first two times, Graham had told Fred, "You are not ready, my son." On the third occasion, he stared at Coinbase's performance—still growing up and to the right—and gave his blessing for a Series A funding round, introducing Brian and Fred to his well-heeled network of money men.

But despite Graham's endorsement and Coinbase's growth numbers, the venture capital world—normally so risk-loving—was still skittish. Most VCs didn't understand bitcoin, and many of those who did saw something that would invariably be snuffed out by law enforcement. The biggest exception was Fred Wilson, who persuaded the other partners at Union Square Ventures to take a trip to San Francisco for a serious look at Coinbase's potential. If all went well, the firm would lay down $5 million.

Now, on this fateful May morning, Wilson had called in sick. Brian and Fred would instead have to make their case to Wilson's skeptical compatriots, including Brad Burnham, the cofounder of Union Square Ventures and an open skeptic of bitcoin. "So fucked," thought Brian, again.

Only half-fucked, it turns out. Brian and Fred's presentation, their clean-cut appearance, and Coinbase's up-and-to-the-right trajectory persuaded the Wilson-less Union Square Ventures team to buy in—at $2.5 million. They'd have to find the other $2.5 somewhere else.

For that, a white knight appeared in the form of Micky Malka, who ran the VC firm Ribbit Capital, and for whom bitcoin was deeply personal. Malka, a tall man with protruding ears and close-cropped hair, speaks with a heavy Latin accent of his native Venezuela, where he had seen firsthand how a venal, inept government could debase a money supply. Like so many bitcoin believers, Malka saw digital currency as a torch for economic freedom that autocrats like

Hugo Chavez, Venezuela's ruinous leader, could not snuff out. "He could see the global money angle and for him, unlike other investors at the time, bitcoin was not heretical," says Fred.

For Malka, a bet on Coinbase was a bet on bitcoin, and he could not say no. Coinbase had its full Series A.

As lawyers put the final touches on the deal, Fred recalled how a friend at Goldman Sachs had made him a promise. One of the bank's few senior directors who shared Fred's frustration with Goldman's dithering digital ways, the friend told him he would cut a $25,000 check to invest in anything he pursued. Fred called and asked if he still meant it. He did. And so, as Goldman Sachs sat on the sidelines while bitcoin blossomed, at least one of its executives made out like a bandit as his $25,000 early stake morphed into Coinbase stock worth millions years later.

Not everyone thought so highly of Coinbase's Series A round. Sam Biddle of Valleywag, a now defunct muckraking site, greeted the funding news with a sneering headline: "VC Dumps $5 million in real dollars into bitcoin hysteria." He also pooh-poohed bitcoin itself, grousing, "We're all talking about it because an obscure, obfuscating group of libertarian nerds are gaga for the digital currency."

The *Wall Street Journal*, the country's business newspaper of record, took a more upbeat tone. In a long article, the paper noted the $5 million investment as a landmark moment for cryptocurrency and quoted an effusive Fred Wilson, who praised Coinbase as the "JP Morgan of bitcoin." Brian and Fred high-fived and went back to work.

• • •

The Bluxome Street place Brian had rented across from The Creamery was actually a two-floor, one-bedroom apartment, but after the Series

A round, it started to resemble an office—and also a cult of bitcoin. Fred had taped up an iconic "Dream" poster of the rapper Biggie Smalls, but changed the "d" to a "b" so it read "Bream," short for "Bitcoin Rules Everything Around Me." And occupying pride of place sat a wood-and-glass cube containing a bright blue betta fish named Satoshi.

The apartment-turned-office was filling up with people too. After Olaf came Craig Hammell, a talented engineer who had helped build the dating site OK Cupid—perhaps a fitting career choice for someone so painfully shy with women that he didn't have a girlfriend until his senior year of college. Brian and Fred had met Craig on a trip to New York and, discovering he was a bitcoin believer, invited him to San Francisco for a work trial. Upon arriving, Craig moved into "Hacker House," a place that billed itself as a home for the city's tech elite, but for Craig was more of a hustle than a hot spot.

"I realized it was a way to rip off people by getting them to pay $1,500 a month to live with nine other guys in a crummy apartment," Craig recalls. Soon after, the building's owner discovered what was going on and evicted everyone, including Craig. So he grabbed his sleeping bag and moved into Bluxome Street for the next few months, coding late into the night and rising early to shower and code some more. For someone who, in Olaf's words, "is an insane workhorse who just loved to ship coin," a round-the-clock bitcoin gig suited Craig just fine. Like Olaf, he took his salary in bitcoin, and also like Olaf, he had been an early client of the company—Coinbase customer number 80.

Years later, Olaf—now fabulously wealthy—would distill his Coinbase experience into a nugget of advice for startups: *Hire your customers.* In Olaf's view, Coinbase flourished even as dozens of other bitcoin startups flamed out because it hired people who believed in the company and loved bitcoin. It's good advice, and not just for crypto companies. Phil Knight, the legendary founder of Nike, laid the foundation of his shoe empire with a small team of devout sneakerheads.

Unfortunately for Brian, not all of his customers wanted to work at Coinbase. One who said "no thanks" was Julian Langschaedel, a superb coder who lived in Germany. For months, Brian had paid him to help adapt Satoshi's original bitcoin code—which was designed for individuals to run on home laptops—into something sturdy enough to serve Coinbase's commercial purposes. Fred and Brian persuaded Julian to come to San Francisco for a work trial. These work trials were part of Coinbase culture and amounted to a several-days test to see if a prospective employee would fit in. Julian fit in just fine but, for his part, he had two objections. The first was that Americans worked too much. He preferred a work culture that left more time for sipping beer. Julian's other objection was the beer itself—more specifically, that Americans did not know how to make it right. He flew back to Germany.

Coinbase had better luck with Charlie Lee. A stout, soft-spoken man who wears his jet-black hair in a sharp part, Lee had used his "20% time" at Google—a renowned perk that let employees spend a fifth of their work hours on personal projects—to create Litecoin, an early alternative to bitcoin. Charlie's entire life had been shaped by his extraordinary proficiency at math. This included his first day of elementary school in Ivory Coast, where a teacher discerned that first-grade mathematics was too easy for Charlie and promoted him to the second grade. The second-grade teacher, however, drew the same conclusion and, the following day, Charlie walked into the math class of the third grade.

"I'm Asian, so I was already one of the smaller kids, but walking into that third-grade class, I was smaller than ever," he recalls.

As he grew older, Charlie's talent served him well, helping him build computers with his brother Bobby before he was a teenager, and later as an engineer at Google, where he worked on building YouTube and the operating system for Google's web browser, Chrome. Charlie applied his math skills to engineering but also to economics, which led him to become a gold bug—a quirky class of investors that regards the yellow metal as better value than stocks or bonds. He was a gold bug until 2011, when he discovered bitcoin.

"It really made sense to me. I read the code part and realized it would be big. I decided to go all in during 2013. It was a better version of gold," he said. Charlie meant it, barely blinking when the value of his first bitcoin investments dropped from $30 to $2 in 2011—one of many spectacular crashes that would help define the currency in its early years. By 2013, he not had only put all his own money into bitcoin but urged his family to do the same. His brother didn't need much persuasion—Bobby Lee was by now becoming fabulously wealthy by founding China's first bitcoin exchange.

Getting ordinary people to buy bitcoin, however, was a tall order. Charlie shared Brian's view that the rigmarole of wallets and private keys was too daunting for non-technical people, and that it couldn't go mainstream without a service like Coinbase. He became Coinbase's third hire.

The small team—Brian, Fred, Olaf, Craig, and Charlie—quickly developed an esprit de corps, hitting a local rock-climbing gym and unwinding over *Call of Duty* and other video games—matches that pitted Fred, the national gaming champion, against two or even three of the others. But mostly the Coinbase crew worked like maniacs. They treated the task of building the startup with the urgency of a military operation, coding the website from morning until 10 or 11 at night, then pausing to sketch grand schemes on whiteboards, then returning to their laptops to code some more. High on startup endorphins, the early Coinbase team followed Fred's lead. Fiercely competitive, the former lacrosse and basketball star took to bellowing about "running through brick walls" until the phrase became a company mantra that can be found on Coinbase's website to this day.

One such brick wall came in the form of Apple. A teenage bitcoin enthusiast had built an app for Coinbase as a quick way for customers to buy and sell bitcoin on iPhones. Unfortunately, Apple didn't allow cryptocurrency trading and would bar any apps that offered it from its App Store. Brian, though, came up with a plan to run right through this wall: Coinbase would use a technology called geo-fencing to disable the app's trading feature, but only for the town of Cupertino, California—the site of Apple's headquarters and where its engineers vetted new apps. As far as those engineers could tell, Coinbase's app complied with policy, and so it was allowed to remain in the App Store. Meanwhile, Coinbase customers in the rest of the country began slinging bitcoin on their iPhones.

It was a neat trick and a textbook example of how to run through a brick wall. Unfortunately for the Coinbase crew, other walls were too strong to bust. Two obstacles in particular loomed that could not only halt Coinbase's progress but kill it outright. The first was a serious hacking attack of the sort that had already wiped out numerous other crypto startups. The second was the US government. Coinbase came perilously close to being crushed by both.

. . .

The hacking attack came in mid-2013 when the Coinbase team had paused to eat dinner. An odd email alert notified Fred about a withdrawal from Coinbase's hot wallet—the place where the company stored millions of bitcoin to handle day-to-day transactions. It had to be a mistake, he thought. Coinbase guarded the keys to the hot wallet in the way a bank protects its vault and Coke protects its secret formula. No intruder could come anywhere near it. Then came the notification of a second withdrawal.

"Shit. Better check this out," Fred told Charlie, who had his laptop at hand during dinner.

Charlie logged in to the Coinbase control screen, and what he saw made his heart sink. Someone else had logged in and was siphoning out the company's bitcoin. Worse, the intruder was growing bolder—and greedier. The initial theft had been for only a few bitcoin, but now the hacker was plundering Coinbase wallet in earnest. After the third illicit withdrawal, Charlie frantically changed the password to access the wallet and shut off access to everyone else, but not before the mysterious robber had helped himself to a hoard of bitcoin. The Coinbase crew glumly finished dinner, their startup $250,000 poorer than when the meal began.

The team quickly figured out what had happened. The thieves, it turned out, had hacked one of Coinbase's IT contractors to obtain the password—an all-too-common trick in the cybersecurity world, where hackers treat external vendors as the soft white underbelly into a company's network. Brian ordered a security overhaul, requiring any firm that worked with Coinbase to use a Chromebook laptop provided by the company. He also took stock of what had happened.

The robbery delivered a financial hit, of course. But it also posed an existential threat to Coinbase's reputation if anyone found out. In those go-go early days of bitcoin, when hacks and scams were everywhere, Brian had branded Coinbase as a safe and secure alternative—a place where customers could park their funds with the same confidence as at a big bank. A media headline blaring that Coinbase could not protect its own assets would be devastating. Banks that lose your money don't stay banks for long. Fortunately, no one spilled the news about the hack, leaving Brian and the others to return to doing what they did best: work their asses off.

Still, the robbery left uncomfortable questions hanging over the team. The hacker had gotten into Coinbase's hot wallet, which was connected to the internet, but the company had millions more in bitcoin stashed in "cold storage"—how crypto people refer to bitcoin stored on physical devices like USB keys or even scraps of paper. These techniques meant the all-important private key for a given bitcoin wallet was stored off the internet so hackers couldn't steal it. The obvious appeal of cold storage meant there was a growing market for stashing private keys offline. One company, Xapo, even offered a service that stored customers' private keys in a vault under a mountain in the Swiss Alps.

Coinbase's own cold storage system was hardly that dramatic. In the early days, for instance, a chunk of customer bitcoin resided on a USB drive in Brian's pocket. This produced some uncomfortable moments, most notably when Brian arrived at US Customs after a trip overseas. In response to a standard question from a customs agent about whether he was entering the US with more than $10,000 in cash or cash equivalents, Brian decided to say no. Better not to tell the agent about the USB stick on his key ring holding millions of dollars in bitcoin.

As Coinbase grew, it quickly added other layers to its cold storage, including a multicity system where private keys were broken into different segments and scattered across the country. Similar to the Horcrux puzzle in the Harry Potter series, the system relied on different people finding and reassembling the different pieces in order to re-create a private key that held a store of bitcoin. It was a clever way to guard Coinbase's reserve supplies, but in the wake of the hack of the company's hot wallet, Brian and the others felt less confident.

In response, the company hired Andreas Antonopoulos, a well-respected bitcoin scholar, to carry out an audit of its cold storage supplies. Using a series of random samples, Antonopoulos tested whether the private keys scattered across the country actually unlocked the supply of bitcoin they were supposed to hold. Brian breathed a lot easier when Antonopoulos's audit came out clean.

Hackers conducting out-and-out robberies were, however, just one of the species of criminals who confronted Coinbase. Far more common were the fraudsters who used trickery rather than hacking to steal bitcoin. In a common scam, these crooks purchased stolen bank account credentials from sketchy sites on the internet and then signed up as Coinbase customers. They then purchased bitcoin using funds from the ill-gotten bank accounts in the hopes of whisking the bitcoin to another wallet before the bank or Coinbase had figured out what occurred. For Coinbase, such scams were a double disaster—not only did the company lose bitcoin, but the bank would restore the victimized customer's loss by clawing back the funds Coinbase had received.

A variation of this scam involved crooks who bought bitcoin despite not having funds in their bank account to pay Coinbase. At the outset, Coinbase made customers wait three days before delivering the bitcoin a customer had purchased—the amount of time it took to confirm, under the banking system, whether the customer indeed had the requisite funds. Brian, however, believed Coinbase had an opportunity to turbocharge its business by offering customers same-day service, delivering bitcoin within an hour. Despite entreaties by Craig and Olaf, who warned the plan would be a scammers' bonanza, Brian pushed forward. Big mistake. It took less than a day to realize the same-day service was a fiasco as fully 10 percent of the company's transactions came back as fraudulent, costing Coinbase both cash and bitcoin. The team wryly referred to the problem as "friendly fraud."

The team also had to grapple with the uncomfortable fact that some of their customers treated the company as their personal money-laundering agent for a host of crimes. These included ransomware operators who would lock up the computers of companies, cities, and schools and only unlock them once the victims had paid a ransom in bitcoin. Once crooks had collected their ransoms, a site like Coinbase offered an excellent place to turn those bitcoin into US dollars.

Coinbase was hardly the first company to be an unwitting agent to money laundering. Extortionists and drug dealers have long used money-transfer services like Western Union and even Apple gift cards as a way to move their ill-gotten loot. But unlike Western Union and Apple, Coinbase did not enjoy decades of goodwill. Worse, it dealt in bitcoin, already a red flag. If criminals ran rampant on Coinbase, a host of powerful agencies would waste no time shutting it down.

Olaf, already swamped with thousands of customer support tickets, did his best to squelch the crooks who crawled like cockroaches from one Coinbase account to another. If he saw activity that looked like money laundering, he would cut off the offending customer and file a document called a "Suspicious Activity Report" with the US Treasury, a process he later described as "covering your ass."

The process worked for a while, keeping Coinbase in the good graces of law enforcement, if only barely. For his part, Fred Wilson had seen enough. The company's mercurial patron warned Brian and Fred that running through brick walls was well and good, but not when it came to federal regulators like the US Secret Service and the Financial Crimes Enforcement Network. Coinbase needed adult supervision in the form of a compliance officer, whether the founders wanted one or not.

And so Martine Niejadlik joined Coinbase in the fall of 2013 as hire number four. A tell-it-to-you-straight New Yorker with a bushel of frizzy hair, Martine was a veteran of an earlier generation of financial startups, including PayPal, and she had helped develop the famous credit metric known as the FICO score. Along with her real-world experience, she also stirred the first strain of diversity into Coinbase's bro-centric culture: she was the first woman, the first parent, and the first forty-something. Fred Wilson had personally persuaded her to join, emphasizing how the bitcoin startup was on the path to rocket-ship growth, and it needed Martine to keep it steady.

. . .

Adam White had not been on a rocket ship before, but he had been on plenty of fighter jets. The onetime US Air Force commander had carried out dozens of F-16 missions over Iraq and Afghanistan, and despite his mild-mannered demeanor, he brought an insatiable intensity to any task. After an initial rejection letter from Harvard Business School, he slashed his sleeping schedule to four hours a night while in the Air Force in order to prepare seventy-two versions of a second application.

That did the trick. He got into Harvard but, as an early bitcoin believer, he discovered to his dismay that no one leading the prestigious B-school had any time for cryptocurrency. "It was supposed to be the West Point of capitalism, so I found it strange that the idea of a private system of money didn't go over well. I tried to write about bitcoin for one of my economics papers, and my professor told me not to," he recalls.

Upon graduation, Adam followed the predictable path of other business school graduates, doing a stint at Bain & Company, and then as a product manager at a video game company. But his bitcoin fever kept burning.

When he turned up at Coinbase, Fred and Brian—true to form—put him through his paces with an elaborate logic riddle. This one involved people stranded on an island who could leave only if they could guess their own eye color based on a clue from a green-eyed guru. Adam, realizing the problem turned on deductive reasoning, solved it, leading the Coinbase founders to invite him for a work trial—paid entirely in bitcoin—that required him to sign up local merchants to accept bitcoin payments. It was a tall order, given the digital currency's shaky status in the real world, but Adam was undaunted. With Fred Ehrsam's exhortations about "running through brick walls" ringing in his ears, he sent three hundred cold-pitch emails, tracking the response rate with a spreadsheet. It worked. At the end of his work trial, Adam had persuaded an airline, a frozen yogurt shop, and a social media site to plug their payment systems into Coinbase and accept bitcoin payments.

"You're hired," Fred told him, and turned him loose to sign up more merchants. Adam thrived in the role, signing up ten $1 billion businesses for bitcoin within a year and relishing the workaholic culture. "Coinbase was very hierarchical, like the military," he recalled. "I idolized Fred as a leader. He was the blend of an elite software developer and a Goldman Sachs trader."

Adam's arrival in October of 2013 coincided with a surge of new customers for Coinbase as the company's month-over-month figures kept on their magical trajectory up and to the right. Meanwhile, news of bitcoin was spreading far beyond the tech-y corridors of San Francisco as the mainstream press began to write serious stories about Satoshi's creation. Much of this had to do with the price of bitcoin, which crossed above $100 in the summer of 2013 and kept on climbing. But it also had to do with novelties like bitcoin ATM machines popping up in coffee shops and a growing horde of art and merchandise that signified to everyone a new tribe was in town.

The bitcoin buzz in the air also electrified the Coinbase crew's apartment-turned-office on Bluxome Street as a steady stream of bitcoin pilgrims dropped by. These included people who would go on to become some of the most famous figures in the crypto clique. The venture capitalist Marc Andreessen came by, and so did Tyler and Cameron Winklevoss, the Harvard rowers who took a large legal settlement from Mark Zuckerberg over the founding of Facebook and plowed it into a bitcoin fortune. A visionary and crypto zealot named Balaji Srinivasan turned up. Craig and others thought he looked like a cross between a drug dealer and a street person with his torn Nikes and stained sweatpants, but they became transfixed. Balaji may have looked like a hobo but he sounded like an Ivy League professor, delivering an impromptu lecture on the work of political economist Albert Hirschman. A scrawny teenager named Vitalik Buterin, who would soon invent the most important cryptocurrency after bitcoin, also spent days puttering around the Coinbase office.

Not all visitors to Bluxome Street were so welcome. On several occasions, irate Coinbase customers appeared at the door, demanding explanations for whatever glitch had befallen their account. Olaf or Craig would do their best to assure the customer their bitcoin were safe and nudge them back outside onto the street. On another occasion, a stalker appeared at the door, a young man who explained he had been watching that "very good-looking guy"—Fred—and had obtained the Coinbase address from a burrito delivery person. Would they like to hire him? He, too, was coaxed back outside.

In late 2013, Coinbase also hired its first lawyer, Juan Suarez. A boyish-looking twenty-five-year-old with deep-set eyes and a mop of dark hair, Suarez had clerked for future Supreme Court Justice Neil Gorsuch and was following the cookie-cutter career path lawyers call Big Law. Bored out of his mind by long days reviewing subprime mortgage documents, Suarez spent his nights lurking on Reddit forums and reading about bitcoin. When he saw that Coinbase was hiring, he recognized his deliverance. "I was writing this multidistrict litigation bullshit over Countrywide mortgages, so I thought 'screw it.' I put together this half-assed slide deck on how I could help Coinbase. Martine told me she had received many more-qualified applications but liked my deck," he recalls.

Together, Martine and Juan began to impose some order on Coinbase's cavalier approach to legal and financial filings. They also commenced a series of diplomatic visits to the Secret Service, the FBI, Homeland Security, and other powerful agencies, explaining the potential of bitcoin and assuring them Coinbase wasn't a money-laundering front. Encountering unexpected allies like the prosecutor Katie Haun, their message started to resonate, and Coinbase began to acquire a faint halo of respectability.

Presiding over all of this like a pair of drill instructors stood Brian and Fred. Hunkered in a command center on the upper floor of the Bluxome apartment, the pair radiated workaholic energy. If Fred's mantra was "running through brick walls," Brian's was "headphones on." The Coinbase crew would see Brian's bald head encased in giant cans, a signal to stay away. "Brian had this 'don't fucking bother me' vibe when the headphones were on. Don't even walk past him when he's in the zone," Juan recalls.

Coinbase's cold and non-fuzzy culture would later lead *Bloomberg Businessweek* to describe Brian and Fred as "Vulcan Swiss bankers . . . do not try to make them laugh." Meanwhile, the company's already arduous hiring culture—with its sink-or-swim work trials and Google-style interview riddles—became more intense still with a practice called "doing the thumbs." This entailed everyone who had inter-viewed a prospective hire meeting in a room and at once engaging in a Gladiator-style display of up-or-down. A single thumbs-down typically doomed a candidate.

For Juan, the Coinbase culture could be extreme, but it didn't faze him. "I thought it was fun. If you want to talk about a 'cold and Dickensian' culture, try working in a big law firm," he says.

Nonetheless, Fred and Brian's imperious approach to managing began to leave other Coinbase employees edgy and exhausted. Fred's relentless exhortation to run through brick walls, at first inspiring, became intimidating, and the startup risked collapsing under its own intensity.

Then, in December of 2013, came Nathalie McGrath, a soulful young woman with kind blue eyes and a tumble of brown hair. Nathalie had cut her professional teeth running operations and manning the front desk for the MBA program at Stanford University—a place populated with the same hard-charging, bro-ish strivers she found on Bluxome Street. At her Coinbase interview, Brian and Fred promptly served up a crushing logic problem that involved a cruel Pharaoh forcing his subjects to choose from a jar of black or white marbles. The wrong choice meant death. When Nathalie asked them why the Pharaoh was doing this in the first place—a question outside the scope of the problem—an impatient Brian replied that "the slaves are rebelling and we need to set an example."

"Well, I would push the marbles aside and make the slaves more productive," Nathalie replied. Fred declared this to be bullshit. But Brian liked the answer and decided such unconventional thinking should be rewarded. Soon after Nathalie was hired. She and Juan Suarez came as hires number six and seven.

Coinbase had everything a startup needed—money and mentors and hard-driving coders—except for one thing. The company, like so many in the Valley, lacked emotional intelligence. With Nathalie's arrival as chief of staff, that began to change.

Tasked with organizing Coinbase's first retreat, Nathalie deftly deflected Brian and Fred's idea that they do a "hunt and gather" outing that would require every employee to kill their own food. Instead, Nathalie arranged a trip to Napa Valley and several days of team games sandwiched between bouts of boozing and hot tubs.

The outing worked. Nathalie's subtle ministrations smoothed over the gruffest parts of the company, and the Coinbase crew began to click like never before. Even the two Vulcan bankers expanded their emotional depth—albeit often with each other. Years later, Fred would recall how he and Brian took their bromance to a new level during a trip to Oahu, where together they went over a set of thirty-six questions presented in a *New York Times* article as a way to accelerate intimacy.

Meanwhile, the startup's monthly numbers, ever up and to the right, began to resemble another sacred Silicon Valley invocation—the hockey stick. The phrase "hockey stick growth" implies a sudden lurch upward, and this is what Coinbase had toward the end of 2013, as the company rapidly approached a customer count of one million wallets. Fueling it all was a staggering jump in the price of bitcoin, which burst past $200 in October, then $500 in November, and over $1,000 in December. The first truly big bitcoin boom was in full swing. And Coinbase, which had sweated to raise a $5 million Series A at the start of the year, now had the top venture capitalists of Silicon Valley lining up to throw money at them. So they took it. Days before 2013 came to an end, just over a year since opening for business, Coinbase closed a $25 million Series B round, by far the biggest-ever investment in crypto. It was time to celebrate.

· · ·

"Bang!" "Bang!" The bullets tore through targets at a shooting range in South San Francisco. Brian and the rest of the Coinbase crew yelped with delight when their shots hit the mark, and with an exhilaration of being at the top of the cryptocurrency world. Martine, the compliance officer, stood firing guns alongside her Coinbase colleagues. There on the shooting platform, she listened to the bark of the pistol reports when suddenly, she felt a searing spot on her cheek. A hot shell casing had whizzed out of a gun and singed her. Was this a sign?

4

Bust

The sun rose over the hills dotted with oak trees east of San Francisco on a clear and chilly morning. It was New Year's Day 2014, a year that would bring the disgrace of comedian Bill Cosby and the appointment of Janet Yellen as the first woman to head the Federal Reserve. Overseas, the US was confronting the rise of a terrorist group called ISIS, while at home, gay couples filed court appeals for the right to marry. In Silicon Valley, tech investors made their first investments in a mattress-in-a-box company called Casper and a quirky work tool call Slack, while *Forbes* magazine would hail a ride-hailing service called Uber as one of the hottest startups of the year. And as Brian and the Coinbase crew shook off their New Year's hangovers, San Francisco still buzzed about bitcoin.

The digital currency had pulled back from its giddy high of $1,100 in December, but still bounced around near $800—an astonishing development given that one bitcoin had sold for $13 at the start of 2013. Better yet, the regulatory cloud around bitcoin had started to lift after a lawyer named Patrick Murck had testified before the US Senate in November of that year about the benefits of a decentralized digital currency. To the surprise of many, the senators expressed interest and even encouragement about bitcoin. For Murck, who testified as general counsel of a new group called the Bitcoin Foundation, the hearing was the culmination of a year's hard work. Murck and an oddball assortment of other bitcoin advocates had launched the foundation as a sort of crypto chamber of commerce, pushing to bestow an air of respectability on Satoshi's creation.

It was not just bitcoin flourishing. Other cryptocurrencies had emerged with fan bases of their own and, like bitcoin, could be exchanged for real-world money. These included Litecoin, the offshoot of bitcoin created by Coinbase's Charlie Lee, but also off-the-wall creations like Dogecoin—a novelty currency inspired by a feel-good meme about a Shiba Inu dog, but which nonetheless became worth tens of millions in real-world dollars. Meanwhile, a visionary programmer named Jed McCaleb, who'd founded the world's biggest crypto exchange, helped launch a versatile currency called Ripple before hatching another one called Stellar. Today, Ripple and Stellar are together worth over $10 billion.

Meanwhile, competition had come for Coinbase. Barry Silbert, the company's early investor, launched a company called Grayscale that sold bitcoin in the form of shares in a trust, which allowed investment funds—whose bylaws forbade them from buying it directly—to acquire exposure to bitcoin. That wasn't all. Cameron and Tyler Winklevoss, the twins who had parlayed their Facebook fortune into a bitcoin hoard, had backed a startup called BitInstant. Like Coinbase, BitInstant offered ordinary consumers an easy on-ramp to the world of crypto as well as a service for merchants to accept bitcoin. Unlike Coinbase's cold, "Vulcan banker" Brian, its CEO was a gadfly twenty-four-year-old with a propensity for hard partying and who sat as a vice chair of the Bitcoin Foundation. And in late 2013, a group of venture capitalists made a big bet on a company called Circle to challenge Coinbase, while Xapo—the service that stored bitcoin under a mountain—launched an easy-to-buy cryptocurrency tool as well.

Even if Coinbase had more competitors than ever before, it hardly mattered during the bitcoin bonanza of early 2014. A flood of first-time bitcoin customers meant the pie was growing and there was enough for everyone. For Coinbase, which took a cut of every purchase, the rush of newbies also meant a surge of revenue. The monthly numbers read way up and way to the right: a 7,000 percent annual increase in customers. Meanwhile, Adam White, the indefatigable fighter jet veteran, persuaded more and more merchants to accept bitcoin. And it was no longer just obscure fro-yo vendors signing up. In a blitz of salesmanship, White also persuaded a series of giants, including Overstock, Expedia, and Dell, to try out cryptocurrency. Not long afterward, he added to the coolness cachet of Coinbase by signing a contract for the company to provide bitcoin services to Burning Man, the drug-fueled techie bacchanalia that takes place in the Nevada desert every August.

All of the merchant sign-ups, combined with the roaring consumer market, meant 2014 should have seen Coinbase post-growth results resembling a hockey stick worthy of Wayne Gretzky.

It didn't happen.

• • •

In early February, a young Frenchman named Mark Karpelès sat in a Tokyo apartment with Tibanne, his orange-and-white tabby cat. He was nervous. A social misfit, he had become famous in crypto circles as MagicalTux, the online handle he used to run Mt. Gox, the biggest bitcoin exchange in the world. He had not started Mt. Gox. That had been the work of the coder Jed McCaleb, who had launched the site to trade cards for the game *Magic: The Gathering*. Hence the name: Mt. Gox stood for Magic the Gathering Online Exchange. But McCaleb soon repurposed the site for users to swap bitcoin rather than cards, before selling Mt. Gox to Karpelès in 2011. Karpelès, despite his awkwardness, built Mt. Gox into a colossus, accepting wire transfers from across the world as his site became the preeminent destination for bitcoin. He also became a director of the Bitcoin Foundation. By 2013, 70 percent of all bitcoin buying and selling took place on Mt. Gox. But on this February day, Karpelès was nervous—and for a very good reason.

As he sat stroking his cat, a barrage of emails and Reddit messages flared on his computer screen, all asking the same question: *Where is my money?* The messages had been coming at him for days, each wave angrier and more insistent than the last. Karpelès knew the answer to their question. It was simple: the money was gone. And the money was gone because hackers had burrowed into Mt. Gox's servers and drained them of over 740,000 bitcoin—a sum worth over half a billion dollars at the time. The crisis reached a crescendo as a customer named Kolin Burges turned up on the streets of Tokyo for two weeks, holding a sign that read "Mt. Gox, Where Is Our Money?" As panic mounted and prices plunged, Karpelès dithered. Roger Ver, the libertarian known as Bitcoin Jesus, flew in on a Friday offering to help Karpelès salvage the mess, but, to his dismay, Karpelès proposed chilling out for the weekend and sorting out the mess on Monday. Barry Silbert, the early Coinbase investor, at one point received a call asking if he would like to buy Mt. Gox. He declined.

"I saw they were insolvent. I called the FBI," recalls Silbert.

In another Hail Mary move, those working with Karpelès frantically passed around a memo describing the disaster that had befallen bitcoin and how it could be mitigated. But on February 24, a prominent bitcoin entrepreneur named Ben Davenport leaked the document to a former banker named Ryan Selkis, who had become an influential crypto blogger under the name Two Bit Idiot. Selkis published it and confirmed to the world Mt. Gox was toast and that many devoted bitcoin holders had been wiped out. The boom was over.

In San Francisco, the Coinbase crew watched the disaster unfold and collectively exhaled in relief, knowing they had made a smart bet to avoid getting wrecked. Like many other bitcoin businesses, Coinbase had relied on Mt. Gox as a source of bitcoin liquidity for day-to-day transactions during most of its first year. The company would run calculations to predict how many bitcoin it would need to satisfy customer demand over a given period of time, obtain the bitcoin from Mt. Gox and, thanks to Fred's Goldman Sachs–born trading genius, even set up hedges to profit on price swings on the pool of bitcoin. The system worked for most of 2013 until, in Olaf's words, "Mt. Gox started getting weird."

Charlie Lee also recalls a series of warning signs that suggested the giant exchange run by the Frenchman and his cat was heading for a Chernobyl-scale meltdown. "Mt. Gox credited $1 million to the Coinbase account that didn't belong to us. It was money created out of thin air because Mt. Gox couldn't read the bitcoin blockchain," he says. "Fred saw something was amiss and got Coinbase out in time."

Not everyone was so fortunate. Just as a big bank's collapse inflicts collateral misery far and wide, the Mt. Gox debacle wiped out companies that relied on the exchange for liquidity, as well as thousands of individual investors. Meanwhile, the price of bitcoin tanked. By early February, it had become clear that the giddy heights of $1,100 in December had been a bubble. The bubble had popped. The collapse of Mt. Gox knocked the price down to near $500, and this was just the beginning of a long, painful slump. It would be years before a bitcoin sold for $1,000 again.

As prices tumbled, so did bitcoin's reputation. The digital currency had enjoyed a brief brush with respectability thanks to the 2013 Senate hearing and the work of the Bitcoin Foundation, which had tried to carry on like an ordinary trade group. But by 2014, the foundation was in disgrace and in disarray. Karpelès resigned as a director in the wake of the Mt. Gox catastrophe, while the blogger Selkis (aka Two Bit Idiot)—who had blown the whistle on the whole thing—demanded that the men serving as the foundation's president and executive chairman quit, too. Selkis blasted the pair for failing to warn the broader bitcoin world about Mt. Gox's impending collapse and accused them of colluding with Karpelès to protect their personal stashes. Meanwhile, another face of the foundation had troubles of his own. Charlie Shrem, the gadfly CEO of Coinbase rival BitInstant, had blown off the advice of the Winklevoss twins to cut out the cocktails and club life and focus on running his bitcoin business. A big part of running such a business was staying on the right side of regulators, but Shrem had ignored this until, returning from a trip to JFK airport, DEA agents greeted him with criminal charges, including money laundering. Shrem would plead guilty to lesser charges and serve over a year in federal prison—just one of a growing number of felons tied to bitcoin.

In May, the Foundation appointed others to beef up its depleted ranks, including a former child star of Disney's Mighty Ducks movies named Brock Pierce. The appointment set off a wave of resignations from other members who were aghast at Pierce's troubled past, which included a lawsuit brought by former employees who alleged that he had used drugs to coerce them into sex when they were minors.

Founded as a bitcoin version of a chamber of commerce, by 2014 the foundation looked much more like a fly-by-night gaggle of crooks and con men. Whatever goodwill the group had built up had been squandered several times over.

Worse, the antics of the bumbling Bitcoin Foundation paled next to what serious criminals were doing with the currency. In late 2013, the media reported the arrest of the Dread Pirate Roberts—the mastermind behind the global drug bazaar known as the Silk Road. In a fit-for-Hollywood moment, disguised FBI agents tackled the Dread Pirate—aka Ross Ulbricht—in a San Francisco library and, critically, snatched away his laptop before he could close the cover and encrypt all the data it contained. The laptop provided oodles of information about Ulbricht's sprawling criminal empire, including the keys to his vast stashes of bitcoin—the currency that had made the Silk Road possible in the first place.

It also led to two more high-profile pelts for star prosecutor Katie Haun. Since the time her boss had asked her to open the FNU LNU file to prosecute bitcoin, Haun had become an expert in digital currency. Not only had she learned the ins and outs of private keys and encryption, she had begun teaching investigators at other agencies, including the IRS and the DEA, about how cryptocurrency worked. Meanwhile, it turned out that two federal agents not only knew about bitcoin, but had been treating it as a way to line their own pockets during the investigation to bring down Silk Road. One of them, Secret Service Special Agent Shaun Bridges, had robbed Silk Road accounts to the tune of at least 1,500 bitcoin—worth over $800,000 at the time—that belonged to the US government. And the DEA's Carl Mark Force IV did something much worse. Force not only stole from Silk Road accounts but sold fake law enforcement tips to the Dread Pirate Roberts while also blackmailing him. And, in a surreal low point, he staged the murder of an informant—charging the Dread Pirate bit-coin for the fake hit, and even sending him gory photographs meant to show the informant's painful death. The corrupt cops made sloppy mistakes, however, such as communicating with the Dread Pirate on their work computers and, in Bridge's case, telling people—including prosecutor Katie Haun—that he was the point person on all things bitcoin for the US government. Haun made easy work of this mess and would eventually help send Bridges and Force to prison—triggering another round of headlines about bitcoin and crime. The dirty agents would not be Haun's last bitcoin-related prosecution. Soon afterward, she would lead an investigation to take down BTC-e, an infamous bitcoin exchange run by a shadowy Russian that served as a money-laundering service for criminals around the world.

The news around bitcoin after the 2013 bubble collapsed was often grim, but there were comic moments too. The most notable one came in March 2014 when *Newsweek* magazine, which had briefly gone out of business, returned to the newsstands with a bitcoin scoop to end all scoops: it had found the identity of Satoshi. In a splashy cover story, the magazine revealed that bitcoin's creator had been hiding in plain sight outside of Los Angeles, and that he was a sixty-four-year-old Japanese-American man named Dorian Satoshi Nakamoto, who lived with his mother. The story led to a swarm of reporters chasing Dorian Nakamoto across the freeways of LA. The ensuing restaurant sit-down with Nakamoto revealed the purported crypto creator did not know the first thing about cryptocurrency. The next day, a long-dormant message board account tied to the real Satoshi sent out a simple mes-sage: "I am not Dorian Nakamoto."

Newsweek's credibility lay in tatters as everyone, except the magazine itself, agreed the big bitcoin reveal was a bust. Meanwhile, a group of longtime bitcoin boosters took pity on the hapless Dorian Nakamoto and raised a collection of 67 bitcoin to smooth over his ordeal. Years later, the older man would cash out the donations for hundreds of thousands of dollars, becoming a bitcoin enthusiast himself—turning up as an amiable curiosity at random crypto conferences. And like so much else tied to bitcoin, his puzzled face has become a meme that appears regularly on Twitter and on cryptocurrency message boards.

Nakamoto's adventure brought a comic respite but, by mid-2014, the outlook for bitcoin was bleak. It wasn't just the reputational blows that came with the presence of the Silk Road and its ongoing association with criminality. The bigger problem was that the original promise of bitcoin as a revolutionary new payment method was falling badly short.

While Coinbase and others had made it easier to acquire bitcoin, it was still a headache to spend it in the real world. Even as more merchants accepted the currency, it became obvious to many that it was just a gimmick. Satoshi's invention, it turned out, was a lousy way to pay for things, in part because it could take ten minutes or more to confirm a transaction had cleared. Worse, the price of bitcoin bounced around so much that a consumer's purchasing power might decline by 20 percent in the space of an afternoon. And even as diehards like Olaf endeavored to live on it, ordinary consumers enjoyed an ever-easier number of ways to pay for things—from the quick swipe or tap of a credit card to a nifty new peer-to-peer app called Venmo. Why would someone pay with this slow, sketchy thing called bitcoin?

And any hope people had of bitcoin as an inclusive, democratic form of money was undercut by studies of those using it. Media reports revealed that men accounted for 96 percent of the currency's users—a ratio that was bro-heavy even by Silicon Valley standards. It didn't help that some crypto events featured scantily clad women, representing the worst of the tech industry's "booth babe" culture.

And the price kept dropping. After a brief rally in the early summer, by the fall of 2014, bitcoin fell to $400—and kept falling. By 2015, the price was barely above $200—more than 80 percent off its highs of late 2013.

For many bitcoin believers, including some at Coinbase, which now counted nearly fifty employees, the mood was glum.

But not everyone felt this way. On New Year's Eve of 2014, ten months after the Mt. Gox collapse, Olaf stood outside a party in San Francisco buying bitcoin on his phone. Ecstatic, he told his friends, "Can you believe how cheap it is? It's never going to be this price again."

5

Hard Times

F red and Brian's philosophy of running through brick walls
had served the company well, inspiring employees to pull off
near-impossible feats in the name of growth. But like Facebook, whose early motto was "move fast and break things," Coinbase
would pay a price for its run-and-gun approach. Running through
brick walls is a killer tactic—when it works. When it doesn't, you end
up on your ass—with a bloody nose.

Coinbase's earlier bid to outwit Apple, for instance, had been clever.
It let the startup flout Apple's rules by letting customers buy and sell
bitcoin directly in its app, all the while keeping the iPhone maker in
the dark by disabling the buy-sell feature in the city of Cupertino,
where the app was vetted. But it took Apple only a few months to
discover the ruse, and Coinbase was tossed unceremoniously from
the App Store.

Sometimes when Coinbase crashed through a brick wall, the
founders discovered there was nothing on the other side. That's what

happened after Adam White, the former Air Force captain, made a superhuman effort to sign up dozens of merchants to accept bitcoin—including ten companies with over $1 billion in revenue. Brian and Fred had believed the sign-ups would unlock a gold mine, letting Coinbase take a cut whenever a retailer accepted a bitcoin payment. It sounded grand in theory. In reality, it required a steady stream of customers wishing to buy coffee, furniture, and everything else with bitcoin. That stream was more like a trickle, and then even that dried up. As would happen over and over in coming years, Coinbase's attempt to add a new line of business fell flat.

"The company wanted to be best at all things," Craig Hammell, the shy engineer who was Coinbase's second employee, recalls. "But the brokerage business was always the bread and butter."

The struggle to find diverse business lines was hardly unique to Coinbase. Other tech companies in the Valley—even the biggest—still rely heavily on a core business for the bulk of their revenue, and especially their profits. This includes Google and its parent company, Alphabet, which dabbles in everything from driverless cars to human biology. Most of these bets, though, are money-losing, and it's still search engine advertising that brings in most of the cash that powers Google. Facebook, meanwhile, has failed repeatedly to bring shopping to its platform, and its effort to crack the mobile phone market—in the form of the short-lived Facebook phone—remains one of the company's spectacular flops. The point is that diverse money-making lines are a splendid idea for a company but, as Coinbase was discovering, are very hard to achieve in practice.

In 2015, as the bitcoin bust dragged on, Brian still saw blue skies. It didn't hurt that Coinbase had begun the year with a popping $75 million funding round, which brought the total raised since Brian's time at Y Combinator to $106 million. Among the investors were the usual crowd of venture capitalists, but also a new set of faces from Wall Street—a sign that the traditional world of finance, which had mostly sneered at cryptocurrency, was starting to take bitcoin seriously. Coinbase's backers now included the likes of the New York Stock Exchange, the banking giant USAA, and the former CEO of Citigroup, Vikram Pandit.

Coinbase was also marching into more countries, including more than two dozen in Europe as well as Canada and Singapore. And in a critical move, the company launched a professional exchange. While Coinbase's original retail product let ordinary individuals buy and sell bitcoin, the exchange was a turbocharged version that let big-time traders swoop in and out of positions worth thousands or millions of dollars. To mark the launch, Coinbase staff donned pajamas and stayed up all night for the morning launch of the exchange, code-named Moon Launch—a nod to the crypto world's favorite phrase, "to the moon," which invokes a price run that makes everyone rich. The exchange also promised a new line of business at a time when bitcoin merchant payments had turned out to be a bust. The company's cut, in the form of commission, would be much lower than the 2 percent or so paid by Coinbase retail investors—only 25 basis points, or 0.25 percent. But the trades would be much bigger: A hedge fund buying $1 million of bitcoin would pay Coinbase $2,500. If the exchange caught on, it would mean Coinbase could claim institutional customers in addition to its core base of retail bitcoin buyers.

. . .

A new infusion of investor cash and the launch of a professional exchange was all well and good, but it didn't outweigh the ugly reality that the price of bitcoin remained in the toilet, and that trading volumes had stagnated. Brian, meanwhile, needed to learn how to lead in tough times—and too often, he was a slow learner. His shortcomings were on display during a four-city tour from London to Helsinki that called on him to drum up interest in bitcoin and Coinbase across Europe. It was an uncomfortable experience for a man most at home with his headphones on, face melded with screen, coding like a maniac. Here, he was an introvert doing the job of an extrovert. Being a CEO required selling, schmoozing, and media glad-handing, and Brian disliked all of it. What he liked was building and putting his passion into products.

"The product is never good enough. It often causes me physical pain to think about the state of our product, especially when it's slow, buggy, or inconvenient. It's an obsession," Brian would later write in one of his many blog posts. For an introverted CEO, writing rather than speaking proved the best way to tell his company and his customers what he was thinking.

Normally Fred, the swashbuckling trader, would handle the outside world. But on this trip to Europe, Fred had been tied up with urgent business in the United States, leaving Brian to lead the push alone. As his train pulled into Paris ahead of his appearance at the city's new "Maison du Bitcoin," Brian looked at the overcast skies and felt his energy flag. As he would do more and more as the trip wore on, he retreated to the place he liked best—his private world of "headphones on," where nothing and nobody could disturb him. Going into this inner world—while hardly ideal for drumming up publicity for Coinbase—gave Brian his unusual ability to summon serenity even in the most stressful of situations.

That didn't mean others at Coinbase could do the same. In San Francisco, the mood was growing tense. Coinbase now numbered dozens of employees, and in April, the staff, along with Satoshi the betta fish, finally left the cramped Bluxome Street apartment for a real office on Market Street, the city's main thoroughfare. New corporate digs did little to dispel the gloom as the price of bitcoin fell further and further. Only true bitcoin believers like Olaf and Craig stayed unfazed. "If you looked at any other metric than the price of bitcoin, it gave you a lot of faith and confidence," Craig recalls of the doldrums of 2014 and 2015.

Others' faith was less sturdy. A third of Coinbase's newer employees quit the company in 2015, leading Nathalie to lobby Brian and Fred to conduct a survey of workplace satisfaction. Seeing the results jolted them: employees were anxious, and morale was sinking.

"Fuck morale," Fred snarled in response to the survey. "If you don't believe in bitcoin and this company, you shouldn't be fucking working here." (Years later, Fred, now fantastically wealthy, would look back at the lean times and reflect, "There were a lot of unfortunate folks who lost faith.") But in 2015, Coinbase's board didn't see it Fred's way. Already concerned by the founders' imperious management style—including remarks by Brian like, "If you're not blowing my mind while talking to me, I don't care"—the board reached for a familiar remedy: consultants and coaches. Brian and Fred were hardly the first Silicon Valley executives who needed to smooth out their rough edges, and the company dug deep to train them.

It wasn't that the founders lacked humanity. Longtime Coinbase employees describe Brian and Fred as brusque and unfuzzy, but also compassionate in critical moments. Adam, the Air Force pilot, recalls their kindness as he struggled to work while his mother was losing a battle to cancer. Craig, the shy workhorse, remembers the founders going out of their way to celebrate his birthday. Nonetheless, Brian and Fred's day-to-day demeanor, their expectation that others match their workaholic lifestyle, and their callous dismissal of things like office morale were often brutal, and the Coinbase board was determined to fix that.

Unfortunately, some of the remedies backfired. Brian glommed onto a cultish management fad called "Conscious Leadership" that employees described as a hybrid of New Ageism and a twelve-step recovery program. They compared it, unkindly, to something out of the satirical TV show *Silicon Valley*. In the name of fulfilling a program called "The 15 Commitments," Conscious Leadership encouraged employees to engage in odd language and rituals when confronted with conflicts large and small. These involved approaching colleagues with the phrase "Can I clear with you?" and then presenting a roster of grievances couched in language like: "The facts are these . . ." "The story I told myself was this . . ." "Voices were raised and you were angry! This triggers me."

"The whole thing was a recipe for confusion and passive aggression. It can be great for self-actualization, but in the workplace, it's a terrible tool," says Nathalie, who more than once found herself crying in the bathroom over the conflicts rippling through the company.

For Brian, though, Conscious Leadership was ideal. To his engineer's mind, it amounted to an equation for emotions, a way to reduce feelings to a formula. In data-driven Silicon Valley, the mumbo jumbo made perfect sense.

. . .

In 2015, the giddy days of $1,000 bitcoin were a distant memory, and the press and the general public recalled crypto and blockchains as a fad—if they thought of them at all. At Coinbase, the company could take some comfort in its squeaky-clean reputation compared with the rest of the crypto industry—but now a series of events meant even that hung in the balance.

"Coinbase's strategy was to be the white knight of crypto," says the venture capitalist Chris Dixon. That meant engaging in none of the shady stuff that had given bitcoin a bad reputation elsewhere. In an industry oozing with crooked players, Coinbase wanted to stand out as a straight shooter. Looking back years later, the company's first lawyer, Juan Suarez, said the game plan for the company's success was straightforward. "A big strategy didn't win the day for us," he says. "All we had to do was say, 'Don't get hacked, don't break the law, and maintain a banking relationship.'"

Even if the world saw it that way, Brian and Fred knew it wasn't exactly true. Coinbase had already been hacked once, though the company had kept it under wraps. It also blew up a critical banking relationship.

Silicon Valley Bank, which goes by SVB, is sui generis as far as banks go. It's built by and for the entrepreneurial machinations of fast-moving tech startups, and its risk profile looks unlike that of any other bank. It has provided financial lifeblood to tens of thousands of startups. Much like Gringotts Wizarding Bank in the Harry Potter series or the Iron Bank of Braavos in *Game of Thrones*, SVB is run by a particular set of bankers with a code of their own. A startup has no revenue yet? No problem. SVB is built for the needs of the Valley, taking on risky startups other banks wouldn't touch and operating within a tight clique of founders, venture capitalists, and tech incubators.

Still, even with its Valley-centric worldview, SVB wasn't particularly enamored of Coinbase or its promise. It had taken a special nudge from Fred Wilson of Union Square Ventures to get SVB to take its business. From the bank's perch, the problem wasn't Brian or Coinbase's business plan—it was bitcoin. Like the emerging cannabis industry, bitcoin faced perceptions of illegitimacy and genuine, unregulated volatility. Mt. Gox had proven that. More than ever, bankers looked at bitcoin companies like so many unexploded landmines. They operated in a legal netherworld where one wrong move could see a company blow up in a federal criminal investigation. Banks funding the ventures could suffer the collateral damage in the form of massive fines. Better to stay clear altogether.

Silicon Valley Bank had made an exception for Coinbase, in part because of Fred Wilson's endorsement and in part because the company had cast itself as just another tech company. "These are companies that are not software companies, but say they are," says a former Coinbase executive, explaining how the company persuaded SVB to be its banker in the first place.

It had been a coup for Coinbase to get SVB as its bank, but that was just step one. Now, it had to keep SVB happy. The bank had seen its share of mercurial founders and high-risk business ventures, but Coinbase was operating on the edges of a Bermuda triangle of finance, tech, and regulation—meaning the stakes were far higher for the bank than backing a Valley bro who builds collaboration software.

It's fine to run through brick walls in software development and on the business front, as Brian and Fred did; it's less desirable (especially to your investors) when you do it in the legal and regulatory environments. For Martine Niejadlik, Coinbase's compliance officer, this approach induced ulcers. It fell to her to persuade the hard-charging founders to adopt the tedious, time-consuming steps needed to stay right with Uncle Sam. "It was their first reality check. You can't just transfer funds around the world without anti–money laundering controls," she recalls.

Brian and Fred did not accept the new oversight with grace. The pair, whether they knew it or not, had taken on the truculent approach of billionaire investor and entrepreneur Peter Thiel, who had helped launch PayPal fifteen years earlier. Like Coinbase, PayPal was ahead of its time and, in Thiel's words, was in a race between tech and politics. In such a race, lawyers and compliance officers only slowed you down. When an executive at PayPal told him it was time to hire a big legal team to guide them, Thiel—an attorney himself—shot down the plan. "No, we're not going to hire them," Thiel recalls telling the executive. "They'll just tell us what we can't do. So we have to just go ahead and not hire the lawyers and just do it."

Thiel's approach during PayPal's early days very much resembled the "running through brick walls" ethos at Coinbase. But there was a critical difference. As Thiel himself has noted, PayPal was built before 9/11 and the Patriot Act—when government scrutiny of banking was much less stringent.

In theory, this meant Brian and Fred had to heed Martine but, in practice, the outcome was a series of blowups, each playing out in roughly the same way. Martine would discover some potentially damaging choice that could spook regulators and would call for measures to get Coinbase on the right side of US banking laws. Brian, who still took his gut-checks from the chatter on Reddit forums, would push back and ask if such steps amounted to a betrayal of bitcoin.

It didn't help that Martine's corner of the company—compliance—was a cost center that didn't create customers or products. She built brick walls rather than running through them.

Martine couldn't stop Brian and Fred from making a series of public gaffes that began to dull Coinbase's once-shiny halo. This included them jumping the regulatory gun by announcing that Coinbase would be offering a licensed exchange in numerous states—basically saying their crypto business, which existed in a sort of legal netherworld, would soon have the status of a regular old stock exchange or brokerage. Martine's stomach sank when news of Fred's boast hit her phone while she celebrated her birthday at Disneyland.

The fallout from Fred's comments came fast as California's powerful financial regulator, the Department of Business Oversight, issued a public smackdown in the form of a "consumer alert" about Coinbase. Officials in the state of New York piled on, telling the *New York Times* that—contrary to Fred's claims—the company had been operating without a license.

Worse was soon to come. Fred had created a PowerPoint deck for investors that highlighted four benefits of bitcoin, including the obvious ones like low transaction costs and a reduced risk of fraud. But the first bullet on that list explained that bitcoin was "immune to country-specific sanctions," citing Russia as an example. This may have been true—governments in many cases could not stop the flow of bitcoin—but advertising this on a company slide amounted to saying, "Our product can subvert US banking sanctions."

It didn't take long for someone to leak Fred's deck to the press. Conservative media outlet *The Washington Free Beacon* published the presentation in February under a blaring headline of how Coinbase was touting cryptocurrency as a tool to circumvent sanctions on Iran. With a single bullet point, Fred had jerked Coinbase into geopolitics.

Silicon Valley Bank had seen enough. Its lawyers had been watching Coinbase closely, and, in the course of a semiannual risk review in the spring of 2015, Coinbase was cut off. No more bank account, no more lines of credit, no more help. For Coinbase, it was an unparalleled disaster, as operating a cryptocurrency service without a bank would be like selling ice cream without a freezer. For one longtime investor and adviser to Coinbase, the bank's move was an unexpected gut-punch, leaving him feeling angry and betrayed.

SVB extended one lifeline to Coinbase, giving the company a six-month grace period to find another bank, which it was able to do, but just barely. "Silicon Valley Bank cutting us off was an existential moment for sure," Olaf says, recalling days of shell shock and tumult in the Coinbase office. It also led the long-running tension between Martine and Brian to boil over. She was given an afternoon to pack her stuff and be gone.

. . .

Coinbase had started 2015 ready for its rocket-ship ride to resume, but by the end of the year, the company felt more like an old Chevy stuck in neutral. Coinbase's board members grew antsy and they pushed Brian to pivot. The word *pivot* is another popular Silicon Valley term and is short for "What we're doing isn't working, so let's try something else." In some cases, it works out spectacularly. Slack, for instance, was a failing video game site before pivoting to become a multibillion-dollar office messaging platform while Airbnb started out trying to offer housing for conferences. More often, however, a pivot is just one last gasp before a startup collapses.

In the case of Coinbase, the board wanted Coinbase to pivot into enterprise blockchain—a crypto flavor-of-the-month that saw companies like IBM and Microsoft offer up privatized versions of bitcoin's famous ledger technology. These amounted to a "members only" blockchain, controlled by a handful of companies, that could create a tamper-proof record of transactions without creating or using a currency.

Brian flat-out refused. He had started Coinbase to spread Satoshi's vision of a new type of money run on a permission-free global ledger— not to build corporate databases. If bitcoin was an unbridled stallion galloping over a wild meadow, enterprise blockchain was a wooden horse going up and down on a carousel. Better for Coinbase to fail, Brian thought, than sign up for that.

Unfortunately, no amount of idealism would help Coinbase make payroll. The company had already seen 35 percent of its engineers grow disillusioned and quit in search of the next hot Silicon Valley thing. And now, as 2015 drew to a close, the company would have to cut some of those who were left. Brian and Fred had always managed Coinbase's finances to allow for a two-year cash cushion if things got bad, and now that window was shrinking fast. In a grim meeting, they realized they would run out of runway unless they cut 40 percent of staff. Any other option would require a miracle. In the waning days of 2015, Brian and Fred sat in the Coinbase tower on Market Street drawing up a long list of candidates for layoff. This wouldn't be mere trimming but an emergency amputation to keep the company solvent. But something gave them pause.

In late October, the price of bitcoin had broken $300 for the first time that year, and in November, it hit $400 before swooning 25 percent. Then in December, when it climbed again to nearly $500, Brian and Fred realized the miracle they needed had arrived. Higher prices meant higher commissions for Coinbase and more money in the bank. Better yet, bitcoin's latest run brought a spate of attention in the media and a stampede of new customers for Coinbase. Brian and Fred could delete the layoff list. Bitcoin was back, and the mood in the Coinbase office grew giddy.

6

Civil War

The long-awaited rebound in bitcoin's prices, which continued into early 2016, brought delighted relief to Coinbase. But outside, in the broader world of cryptocurrency, something ugly was brewing as the tribal factions who were the bedrock of bitcoin turned on each other—and on Brian—like never before. The return of prosperity should have been a cause for celebration, but instead it accelerated a long-simmering conflict.

The source of the conflict was simple: what to do about a bitcoin network that had clogged up. The number of users on the network had grown exponentially, but the infrastructure to support them had stayed the same. This was a problem because more users meant more transactions—transactions that had to be recorded on a block and get added to bitcoin's blockchain to become official. And only so many transactions—typically around two thousand—could fit onto one block. The overflow had to be added to subsequent blocks, which arrived every ten minutes, and this just created a bigger backlog. It was like an ever-growing crowd pouring out of Yankee Stadium and trying to fit into a single subway train.

In the case of Coinbase, the slowdown didn't affect customers who sent bitcoin to another Coinbase account—the site cleared those transactions internally—but any payment to an outside party got stuck in the overflow queue as both parties had to wait for it to appear on the sluggish blockchain. This wasn't a deal breaker for people buying bitcoin as an investment. But for those using bitcoin to buy a cup of coffee, this backlog meant it could take an hour or more for that purchase to clear. Needless to say, only the most diehard crypto believers, like Olaf at Coinbase, who lived on bitcoin for three years, would choose to pay with bitcoin over swiping a credit card, or more recently, "Venmoing" the money—or just handing the barista some cash. The plain truth was that bitcoin was too slow and expensive to catch on with retailers as a practical replacement for cash or credit cards.

Bitcoin insiders had talked for years about this flaw and how to handle "scaling" a service to millions of users; a few of them had put some solutions on the table. An obvious one, endorsed by Brian, was to change bitcoin's code in order to double the size of each block on the blockchain from one megabyte to two, thereby doubling how many transactions get logged at each update. Too many people waiting for the train? Add double-decker cars.

Mathematically, it would have gone a long way to solving the backlog, but one faction of bitcoin coders wasn't having it. Known as Bitcoin Core, they are the most influential of the many tribes in the cryptocurrency community since they maintain and expand Satoshi's original batch of code. These hundred or so developers are the closest thing bitcoin has to a legislature. Generally, when they tweak the bitcoin code, users accept the changes. Notable members include Pieter Wuille, a tousled Belgian with a PhD in computer science, though Wuille and others like to maintain a low profile and operate using a behind-the-scenes consensus to improve the code.

Bitcoin Core objected to bigger blocks because they presented a potential threat to Satoshi's vision for bitcoin—a vision that valued individuals over institutions. In their view, two-megabyte blocks would cost more to mine, thus those who had more to spend, in computing power, would have a leg up. Typically, institutions would have more resources than individuals.

It was a fair point, and the sort of technological spat that would normally get hashed out in committees, op-eds, and PowerPoint presentations. But this was the world of bitcoin, and so it became fervent and religious. The dispute between the big-blockers—those in favor of 2MB blocks—and small-blockers—who opposed them—soon devolved into an online version of salted-earth warfare.

The small-blockers were aggressive. They conspired to get their rivals banned from social media forums where the matter was discussed. Regarding Coinbase as one of the most powerful big-blocker forces, they launched denial-of-service attacks at its servers. They even turned on one of their own by excommunicating Mike Hearn, a former Googler and ally of Satoshi who had been instrumental in building out the bitcoin network in its early days. After his expulsion, Hearn described the situation as open civil war.

Laura Shin, a *Forbes* journalist who would go on to build an influential cryptocurrency podcasting series, wrote of the 2016 war over block size: "Bitcoin Twitter has been a toxic stew of name-calling, trolling, bullying, blocking and threats, with some altercations spanning months, with replies numbering in the hundreds. No tweet or bitcoin Talk comment made by anyone is too old to dredge up and hold against them, no quote from Satoshi Nakamoto too out of context (or fictional) to be used to bolster one's argument."

Brian was a popular—and easy—target. Ideological bitcoin believers had long lambasted him as a sellout for creating Coinbase in the first place—a company that, in their view, should not exist since it didn't give users control over private keys for their wallets, but instead provided a centralized management service. Now that he had become an advocate for big-blockers, zealots had another reason to attack him, and a reason to dredge up their vitriol from the past over centralization.

"A lot of people thought this guy didn't know what he was talking about," says Samson Mow, an executive with the crypto consultancy Blockstream, an ally of the small-blocker Bitcoin Core crowd. "If you look at history, Brian has fallen on his sword again and again to get bigger blocks and failed."

Mow's criticism was civil, if barely. Brian faced far cruder criticisms on social media and on Reddit, a site he read religiously. Unlike most of Silicon Valley, he did not keep up with Techmeme or TechCrunch, two websites that served up industry news and gossip. Brian preferred the hurly-burly of Reddit and Hacker News, sites that encouraged visitors to share headlines and yammer on about their favorite topics, including cryptocurrency. Since the start of Coinbase, Brian and Fred had been eager participants in these debates—explaining and defending the company's decisions and chatting with fans and critics alike. But in 2016, amid the debate over block size, discussions took a darker turn. One popular blockchain forum on Reddit censored Brian and anyone else who supported Coinbase, while anonymous trolls directed hacking attacks at its websites and even death threats at the company's executives.

This was extreme, though safety concerns were nothing new at Coinbase, going back to the days at Bluxome Street when creeps and vagrants would loiter outside. In 2014, the company had hired a bearded tower of a man named Ryan McGeenan, who had served as a security director at Facebook. McGeenan, known at Coinbase as Magoo, served as a bodyguard for Brian and also kept watch over the online threats.

The nature of cryptocurrency meant the entire community was rife with criminals and, as bitcoin grew, so did criminal enterprises within its world. Stories of robbery and kidnapping became more common. Magoo's successor at Coinbase, Philip Martin, was understandably paranoid. "There's innovation in the kidnapping industry. The chances of someone knowing crypto, Coinbase, and being willing to use violence goes up every year," says Martin.

Like many security workers, Martin is a former military man— but also a computer geek who enlisted in counterintelligence after the recruiter promised he would get to play with high-tech software. "Those were damn lies. There were no computers," Martin snorts. Nonetheless, over tours in Africa, Latin America, and Iraq, he eventually got to hone his antihacking skills. At Coinbase, he continued to fight hackers, including those from the money-starved North Korean military, where soldiers turned to bitcoin robbery to support themselves.

To thwart the thieves, Martin developed elaborate security schemes to store Coinbase's crypto reserves. He won't share details for obvious reasons. What is known, though, is the system involves a select group of authorized individuals to assemble and then obtain digital keys wrapped in metal boxes that deflect internet signals. What's more, the keys for accessing bitcoin are scattered across multiple secret locations. "Our philosophy is 'require conspiracies,'" Martin explains, meaning unauthorized access to Coinbase's crypto reserves could arise only through an improbable plot involving multiple people.

But despite all the precautions, violent and uninformed individuals are what Martin fears the most. "I'm most worried about people who know a little bit about crypto but not enough to know there's no room at Coinbase where we keep it," he says.

Brian faced the rising tide of security threats with calm stoicism. At the height of the fight between big-blockers and small-blockers, when his company was being hacked and he was receiving death threats—during what other people were calling a civil war—he described the dispute as bitcoin's equivalent of an election process. But his patience was wearing thin.

At a garish Club Med nightclub in Port St. Lucie, Florida, spotlights swirled and a DJ cranked bad techno music. Inside, Brian sat wearing his customary uniform—jeans and a tight-fitting T-shirt—along with Charlie Lee. The two had come for the Satoshi Roundtable, an annual gathering of dozens of the most influential players in bitcoin. This year's roundtable, in theory at least, had a high-minded purpose: End the civil war. Work out the differences between the big-blockers and small-blockers for the greater good. In reality, it was a bro-fest with multiple nerdy crypto cliques.

A YouTube video from the roundtable captures hours of drunken braying by two self-appointed hosts who conducted faux interviews with equally sloshed participants. It was the worst caricatures of the bitcoin world come to life. Everyone appears awkward and self-important, and the gathering is almost entirely male and mostly white. Brian declined to be interviewed by the hosts. Miffed, they lashed out at him with a cocktail of childish barbs laced with homophobia. "He looks a bit like a penis," they said on their livestream. "He's a beautiful man if you're into penises." And so on.

Brian and Charlie had come to the roundtable in hopes of finding a good-faith solution to bitcoin's intractable scaling problem, but they left feeling hopeless. "Some of the [small-blockers] show very poor communication skills or a lack of maturity," wrote Brian in a blog post after the event. "Being high-IQ is not enough for a team to succeed. You need to make reasonable trade-offs, collaborate, be welcoming, communicate, and be easy to work with."

This was typical Brian, cerebral and unemotional. The blog reflected his habit of setting out his thoughts in writing, where he was most comfortable thinking through ideas (unlike most executives, he did not rely on PR people to write his blog posts). He believed it let him communicate with employees and the public with minimum ambiguity. Unfortunately, the Bitcoin Core crowd didn't care for measured missives, and the vitriol continued unabated on Twitter and Reddit.

"You with your high IQ! You're not being mature and are also not communicating well. You're a central planner and a systemic risk to bitcoin," wrote one Redditor. Another piped up to call Brian's measured essay "retarded." Others joked it was the product of Asperger's, and another group floated conspiracies that Brian was paying individuals to write positive posts. And so it went in the fever swamps of bitcoin social media.

. . .

Shortly after the Satoshi Roundtable debacle, Brian and Charlie embarked on a secret trip to Beijing. Appealing to the Bitcoin Core crowd had proved hopeless, so they hoped to turn to another influential faction to make the case for bigger blocks: Chinese miners.

China had arrived late to the bitcoin scene but, by 2015, had come to dominate mining operations. Deploying massive server farms and cheap labor, Chinese miners used their outsized computing power to win the lion's share of new bitcoin added to the blockchain every ten minutes. This gave them wealth and influence and a big say over the evolving architecture of bitcoin.

A shadowy entrepreneur named Jihan Wu led the Chinese mining faction. He and his associates had drawn on cheap supplies of Chinese coal—often greasing local officials to get it—to power their computer operations and to create massive mining pools. Wu's company also sold computers built with custom chips designed to solve bitcoin's ever-harder algorithms. Wu's empire was a potent economic force and also had political power to sway the block debate. On the outside at least, they appeared to be on the fence.

The debate took place in an upscale hotel room. It included key figures from the Chinese bitcoin economy, including Charlie's brother Bobby Lee, as well as Gavin Andresen, a Massachusetts developer who had worked with Satoshi to build out bitcoin's code in the early days. Brian made his case before the room—poorly, it turns out.

"People in China aren't the type to sit in a room with many people and have an open and vigorous debate," said one of the twenty or so people at the Beijing meeting. "Brian and the other Westerners were all having this open debate while the Chinese were in listening mode. The way in China is to form agreements in small groups and then listen."

Brian's speech came across as overbearing and patronizing. Coinbase was on its way to conquering the US crypto market, but the Chinese entrepreneurs in the room had built bigger exchanges than his, and many had run major bitcoin mining operations to boot. "They're in a much more competitive market," said one person in the room. "China, it's cutthroat, man. A whole other level." And yet Brian was giving them a lecture on how bitcoin should be run. Brian had underestimated—not for the last time, it turned out—the savvy and the clout of Asia's top cryptocurrency players.

Brian and Charlie's secret diplomatic overture to China was a bust. Wu and the other miners continued to side with Bitcoin Core and the small-blockers, and so Coinbase's push for 2MB blocks fizzled out. All Brian had earned for his trouble was frustration and an earful from the trolls on social media.

. . .

The bitter block-size fight of early 2016 never would be resolved. Processing times on bitcoin's blockchain would become even more sluggish—eventually, it would take more than a day to record some transactions. The dream of bitcoin as a popular payment tool was all but dead. But at the same time, a surprise lurked beneath the day-to-day drama over block size: bitcoin's price was bouncing back, and cryptocurrency was flourishing like never before.

As it turned out, the bitcoin evangelists had been right. Cryptocurrency *was* changing the world, just not the way people had thought it would. In the case of bitcoin, Satoshi's creation had failed to upend central banks and the credit card industry, but it had emerged as a bona fide rival to gold.

Just as "gold bugs" hoard the precious yellow metal as a hedge against the collapse of government, people called "hodlers" were hoarding bitcoins for the same reason. The word *hodlers* derives from a drunken bitcoin investor chatting on a message board who errantly wrote, "I AM HODLING" rather than "I am holding." Soon, the term became an essential word in the crypto vocabulary as intrinsic to the dialect as "Lambo" for Lamborghini and "rekt" for obliterated.

In the midst of all this, the various bitcoin tribes took their hands off each other's throats. The civil war hadn't ended, per se, but a détente settled in as cryptos turned their attention to the "gold rush" and getting rich. No sense fighting over transaction times if you're a hodler who's just going to amass a fortune. Hodlers can wait a day for the ledger to update.

. . .

Even more important than bitcoin's bounce back, though, was the appearance of a new digital currency called Ethereum. The idea for Ethereum had been set out in a Satoshi-like white paper in late 2013, a year and a half after Brian had first walked into Y Combinator to build Coinbase. And while the big-blockers and small-blockers of bitcoin traded death threats and invective during 2015, a sunny and unified community of Ethereum backers would share the new currency with the public. Ethereum also enjoyed a special advantage over bitcoin. It had an acknowledged leader in the form of its wunderkind creator who would become the most famous figure in cryptocurrency after Satoshi.

PART TWO

From Boom
to Bubble
to Bust

7

Enter Ethereum

Vitalik Buterin is soft-spoken, pale, and practically skeletal. He likes to wear "My Little Pony"–style T-shirts. A child of Russian émigrés, he grew up in the Toronto suburbs and, even as a tiny boy, knew he was different from other children. Infatuated with numbers, Vitalik had a favorite toy as a small child: it was called Microsoft Excel. In an early photo, a pint-size Vitalik can be seen standing on a chair, gleefully tapping figures into a spreadsheet.

As a teenager, he was eccentric. He wore mismatched Hello Kitty socks and ate lemons, including the rinds. At the urging of his libertarian father, Dmitry, he took an interest in the cryptocurrency called bitcoin. He soon became absorbed. While still in high school, he launched an online news site called *Bitcoin Magazine* as a side hustle, persuading cryptocurrency fans to pay for his lucid essays about digital money and cryptography. Upon finishing high school, Vitalik used the proceeds to travel the world and talk to others with big ideas about bitcoin and how to improve it. He hit Amsterdam, Tel Aviv, and bitcoin's ground zero, San Francisco, where, like many others, he spent a short stint hanging out at Coinbase's Bluxome Street office. He met Charlie Lee, who, recognizing a fellow math genius, invested $10,000 in Vitalik's magazine. During his travels, Vitalik also taught himself to speak Mandarin.

The people he met on his world tour reinforced Vitalik's growing belief there could be a better bitcoin. Like most, he recognized both the elegance and the limitations of Satoshi's creation. The most obvious limitation was its failure to scale. Even after the civil war over block size, the bitcoin network was still choking on too many transactions crammed into too few blocks.

Bitcoin also lacked versatility. The ledger could record transactions and inscribe short messages but could not be programmed to carry out more complicated tasks. Bitcoin's quirky code also presented problems. For a developer to properly get under the hood of bitcoin, he or she needed to learn the computer science equivalent of Ancient Greek or Latin, so complicated was Satoshi's creation.

Chatter in crypto circles said it was time for a Blockchain 2.0—something that could address bitcoin's shortcomings and also push the technology to new frontiers. In 2013, five years after Satoshi published his white paper, Blockchain 2.0 would arrive. Its delivery would come from the mind of a now nineteen-year-old Vitalik, whose own nine-page paper outlined a new blockchain called Ethereum.

Vitalik is soft-spoken and friendly in person and, despite his unusual appearance, no stranger than your average theater geek. But he is a god in the world of crypto. Crypto nerds revere him as "our alien overlord" and "a genius alien who had arrived on this planet to save the world from centralized powers."

At base, Ethereum offers the same thing as bitcoin—digital money and an immutable record. But it also overcomes bitcoin's limitations.

It's faster and allows for "smart contracts," a powerful new type of computing that takes place right on the blockchain.

Smart contracts work like this: Imagine you and I want to place a wager on tomorrow's baseball game. We could put our wager on the Ethereum blockchain in the form of a smart contract. To determine the outcome of the wager, the smart contract needs to consult a neutral and reliable third party to confirm who won the game. In the analog era, such a third-party authority would have been the newspaper or a sports-loving friend. In the world of smart contracts, the authority is a neutral online source known as an *oracle*, and, in our example, could be a website like ESPN or Major League Baseball. In practice, the Ethereum smart contract would consult one of these sites once the game had ended and, as a final step, pay out the wager accordingly.

Thanks to Ethereum, a blockchain could be about much more than digital currency. It was now also a one-stop shop where people could sign contracts over anything from sports wagers to investment agreements to data storage. And instead of lawyers, it was computers that took care of executing the contracts. In this sense, it served as a platform much like what Apple provides developers so they can build apps for its iOS operating system. Ethereum acted just like a crypto operating layer—recording any piece of critical information to its blockchain—and allowing others to build smart contract projects on top of it. And unlike bitcoin, Ethereum offered an easy-to-learn programming language, called Solidity, for anyone who wanted to build applications.

The arrival of smart contracts was a coup for the crypto community—proving that blockchain technology was about much more than a novelty currency—but also came with some staggering real-world implications. Ethereum had the potential to remake any number of financial and legal activities involving contracts, allowing individuals to rely on the blockchain for secure, fast, scalable agreements. Big companies soon sat up and took notice, building their own applications on top of Ethereum. IBM used a version of Ethereum to track customers' identities while Walmart used the blockchain to track pork shipments from China to the United States. Banks experimented with a private version of blockchain to move money back and forth. Even state governments got into the act as Vermont tested putting land titles on a blockchain. The possibilities were endless.

For Vitalik, the flurry of corporate interest was an unintended—and unwelcome—development. For him, the point of Ethereum was not to help big companies make money but rather to disrupt those companies by offering their services on decentralized networks. For instance, rather than storing files on Dropbox or Google, consumers could rely on a network of computers around the world to store them instead, using Ethereum's smart contracts to track everything. Instead of relying on Fidelity or Vanguard, investors could create an automated service on Ethereum to invest and pay out funds according to the terms of a smart contract. In Vitalik's view, Ethereum was not just a new technology but a way to reallocate global power structures.

"Ultimately power is a zero-sum game," he told *Wired* magazine "And if you talk about empowering the little guy, as much as you want to couch it in flowery terminology that makes it sound fluffy and good, you are necessarily disempowering the big guy. And, personally, I say 'Screw the big guy.' They have enough money already."

This wasn't just the stuff of computer nerd fantasies. Shortly after the Ethereum network was up and running, a group of people got together and put $150 million into an investment platform called the DAO. It stood for Decentralized Autonomous Organization, and it entailed turning their money over to a smart contract that would invest in projects based on a formula. The formula took account of how many DAO participants voted for a given project, but the votes—as well as the participants—were anonymous. The entire operation sat as an application on top of Ethereum, and the blockchain would record who owned what and pay out any profits. The project was soon up and running, and computers, informed by the terms of the smart contract, called the shots. Screw the big guy.

Then disaster struck. In June of 2016, two months after the DAO went live, hackers discovered a bug in the program that let them hijack the investment fund and divert part of it to themselves. Within minutes, DAO investors were out $50 million, and under the law of the smart contract, there was no way to recover it. Trusting the machine implicitly creates great efficiency and great possibility, but it dismisses the value of human social arrangements—a common mistake in the tech-utopian world of Silicon Valley where entrepreneurs, in the name of disruption, often fail to account for the harm they can cause for humanity. Facebook connected the world but also undermined democratic elections. YouTube built a massive broadcast system anyone can use but opened a Pandora's box of lies and conspiracy theories. Similarly, the DAO episode managed to demonstrate both the incredible power and the dark side of Vitalik's technology.

There was *one* radical way to rescue the DAO investors: *Go back in time.* The ledger was unchangeable but, if everyone on the ledger agreed, it could be updated to scotch the hacker's heist. That measure required everyone running the Ethereum blockchain to introduce an update that would create a new set of blocks that erased the hackers' ill-gotten gains and returned them to the DAO investors. It was the blockchain equivalent of a constitutional amendment—one that not just changed the law of the land, but also overwrote history so that, in effect, the old law had never existed.

The situation presented a major dilemma for Vitalik, who was torn between saving the DAO—one of the most famous and important early experiments on Ethereum—and preserving the integrity of the blockchain. Ultimately, he agreed to exercise his enormous influence and persuade those running the Ethereum network to rewrite the blockchain, saving the investors. On July 20, 2016, the Ethereum network carried out a "hard fork"—essentially backing the train up to a transfer point, flipping the lever, and sending all the cars down the other tracks.

Most followed Vitalik's lead and recognized the new version of the Ethereum blockchain, but some refused to acknowledge the new order and, staying with the train example, kept on traveling down the original set of tracks. The holdouts argued that code is law, ledger updates are incontrovertible, and no matter the consequences, a human intervention could not be justified. Spurning the hard fork, the splinter group continued to build on the original blockchain, calling it—and the digital currency associated with it—Ethereum Classic. Today, Ethereum and Ethereum Classic operate as separate realms, two versions of what was once one reality. Both are going strong. While the former is forty times more valuable—Ethereum was worth more than $45 billion in mid-2020—both are adding new blocks to their respective chains every fifteen seconds or so.

The DAO debacle briefly damaged Ethereum's credibility, but did little to halt its steady rise as the first serious challenger to bitcoin. The buzz over Vitalik's creation came from the power of smart contracts, but Ethereum had a currency of its own called *ether*, which was mined and traded just like bitcoin. And in a clever piece of design, anyone wishing to run a smart contract had to spend a small sum of ether—known as *gas*—to make it work. This meant it was not just speculators investing in Ethereum, but many software developers who had to pay for it as part of their day-to-day business operations. Ethereum had become akin to a hot piece of real estate where anyone who wanted to run a store had to pay a small tax.

The price began to shoot up like crazy. At the outset of 2016, Ethereum sold for 95 cents and by June the price hit $18. If bitcoin was digital gold, Ethereum was digital silver. Meanwhile, venture capitalists, including Coinbase board member Chris Dixon, had begun to take notice and rave about the potential of Ethereum to change the world. It was like the original 2013 bitcoin mania all over again but this time it was about something much bigger than digital money—Ethereum was a way to change business, the internet, and society itself.

At Coinbase HQ on Market Street, the rise of Ethereum caused excitement—and agitation. Everyone in crypto was buzzing about it, but Brian and others had doubts. They wondered if Ethereum might flame out. Since bitcoin had launched in 2009, a parade of cryptocurrencies had come along, but only bitcoin had shown real staying power. Not only did bitcoin have the status of being first, it had a global network of backers committed to owning it long term. What's more, bitcoin was battle-tested. Hackers had tried for years to find a weakness in its code to steal funds but never succeeded—they had robbed exchanges and individual crypto owners but had never found a way to tamper with bitcoin's all-important ledger. Other cryptocurrencies had been hacked and hijacked. Ethereum wasn't only hacked, but its ledger was tampered with *on purpose*. What's more, buying and selling bitcoin had always been Coinbase's bread and butter—straying from the company's core mission to deal in a still-unproven alternative could bite them in the ass.

Brian's partner Fred Ehrsam didn't see it that way. A trip to Shanghai had convinced him that Ethereum and smart contracts were the future. Ethereum had momentum. It had technology that bitcoin lacked. And unlike bitcoin, Ethereum insiders weren't consumed by civil war.

"Ethereum's core development team is healthy while bitcoin's is dysfunctional," he would write in a blog post, contrasting Vitalik's take-charge ability to the leaderless and toxic state of bitcoin in the wake of the block-size debate. Fred had a point. The shenanigans at the Satoshi Roundtable underscored how "dysfunctional" was the perfect word to describe the clique of high priests overseeing bitcoin's code. And there was no doubt that Ethereum was on a roll as young developers flocked to the new blockchain and whole communities sprang up—including ConsenSys, a Brooklyn-based software foundry—to build around it.

Even if Fred was simply stating the obvious, it didn't mean bitcoin loyalists were above shooting the messenger. Fred's public proclamations about Ethereum triggered the wrath of legions of Twitter and Reddit users, who called him a sellout (again!) and worse—the title of one post in a bitcoin forum denounced Fred as a "Goldman Sachs shill and dirtbag" and other commentators gleefully piled on.

"People hated me because they regard bitcoin in a zero-sum way," recalls Fred. This thinking was stupid, he felt. Throwing support behind Ethereum did not mean betraying bitcoin. The rise of other blockchains meant new opportunities, but bitcoin, even if it was in a rocky phase, still ruled in terms of pedigree and prestige. The crypto universe was expanding, and there would be space for many blockchain projects.

But some people at Coinbase—including Brian—still had to be persuaded. Fred grew antsy as he watched other crypto exchanges add Ethereum while Coinbase dithered. If Coinbase blew off Ethereum, it could be a strategic mistake like those taught in business classes—for example, when Microsoft CEO Steve Ballmer dismissed the arrival of the iPhone. In 2007, a laughing Ballmer infamously predicted Apple would sell none of its new $500 phones while saying Microsoft, safe in its Windows fortress, would control the mobile market. Ballmer's hubris stranded his company for a decade in the tech wilderness. Fred didn't want Coinbase to make a similar mistake.

The debate boiled over during a crowded meeting in the Coinbase office high above San Francisco. Fred embarked on an epic forty-five-minute rant in front of Brian and many longtime employees. The company, he bellowed, had to get on with building Ethereum. Ever the athlete and the alpha male, Fred paced back and forth barking at his colleagues, invoking his favorite phrase, "We're going to do this! We're going to build this! We're going to run through brick walls!"

Fred's restless dynamism carried the day. This came as an immense relief to Olaf, who had watched the rise of Ethereum for months and repeatedly pleaded for Coinbase to add it. Now, the company had finally acted. Ethereum would be a major milestone.

But Olaf would not be a part of it.

• • •

As Coinbase had grown, so had his frustration. The unusual young man from Minnesota had felt at home when the company was a small startup, pulling together for a common cause in a ramshackle office—in some ways, a vibe that wasn't so different from Holden Village, the utopian former logging camp commune he'd left in the Pacific Northwest. But Coinbase had since become bigger and more bureaucratic, which he detested.

Now, as the head of Coinbase's risk management team, Olaf's day-to-day job meant leading dozens of people. This role bored him, and he hated managing people. His mind was swimming with much bigger ideas. The emergence of Ethereum had fascinated him, and so did a host of other cryptocurrency projects that pushed the possibility of smart contracts and other new forms of blockchain technology. It was during this time he hit on what he'd do next. He would launch what even a year before would have sounded inconceivable: a crypto hedge fund to manage hundreds of millions of dollars on behalf of investors. Olaf even had a name: Polychain Capital. And he looked the part—if there was such a thing as a "look" for a crypto hedge fund manager. Traditional hedgies wear suspenders and bespoke suits, but Olaf wore T-shirts or bright tracksuits and styled his blond mane in a baroque feathered coif.

Olaf had to break the news to Brian and Fred. He invited his long-time bosses and two old friends to a 7 p.m. meeting. Sensing what was up, the pair turned their gaze on Olaf: "Just tell us." He did. Brian didn't want to lose Coinbase's first employee and even drafted a letter imploring him to stay before finally accepting that Olaf was determined to ride the next crypto wave on his own. He wished him well. Olaf was the first of Coinbase's early days core team to head out the door. He would not be the last.

. . .

In late May of 2016, Coinbase finally pulled the trigger on announcing it would add Ethereum as a second currency to the professional traders' exchange it had launched the previous year. To mark the moment, the company rebranded the exchange as GDAX, short for Global Digital Asset Exchange. Two months later, Coinbase announced that retail customers would be able to buy and sell Ethereum.

The GDAX launch was cause for celebration at Coinbase, but one with a twinge of "better late than never." During the time the company had deliberated over whether to launch Ethereum, other US exchanges went ahead and just did it. One was Kraken, another San Francisco–based crypto shop run by a fractious, long-haired libertarian named Jesse Powell. In 2015, Kraken had not only offered Ethereum trading but introduced other trading features like margin trading and dark pools (which enabled large buy-and-sell offers in secret), while Coinbase leadership remained preoccupied with the block-size wars. The Winklevoss twins were Ethereum players, too. The pair had learned from their disastrous dealings with BitInstant, whose gadfly CEO had landed in prison. This time, they built a by-the-books crypto exchange called Gemini. Borrowing from the Coinbase playbook, the twins marketed Gemini as a buttoned-up Wall Street business that stayed on the right side of regulators. The new exchange quickly found traction and, like Kraken, offered Ethereum well before Coinbase.

Brian's insight about an open secret—that ordinary people needed an easy way to buy bitcoin—had paved the way for Coinbase's massive early success. It let the company exploit a first-mover advantage to become the go-to service for retail customers to buy bitcoin. Now, as the cryptocurrency world barreled into a new era of Ethereum and institutional investors, Coinbase found itself in an unfamiliar position: late and needing to catch up.

8

Wall Street Comes Calling

Bitcoin first blossomed in Silicon Valley, and it's easy to see why. Only the Valley had the critical mass of libertarian types with tech chops who would embrace something as far-fetched as a global, decentralized system of digital money. The Valley's business culture linking generations of inventors is also perfect for nurturing something like bitcoin. Since the 1930s, this special strip of California has produced entrepreneurs whose work has in turn inspired other entrepreneurs to push technology forward. These include a young Steve Jobs who, when asked why he spent so much time hanging around the semiconductor pioneers of the 1960s, spoke reverently of their magic. "[I] wanted to smell that second wonderful era of the valley, the semiconductor companies leading into the computer. You can't really understand what is going on now unless you understand what came before," the Apple founder told the historian Leslie Berlin.

Bitcoin must also be understood by what came before and, in particular, a group of technologists known as *cypherpunks*. (The word is a portmanteau of *cipher*—meaning coded messages—and *cyberpunk*, the sci-fi genre that combines, as one observer put it, "high tech and low life." Cyberpunk has long been associated with hacker culture.) In 1992, a group of Silicon Valley cypherpunks regularly met at the office of John Gilmore, a software activist and cofounder of the Electronic Frontier Foundation—the web's version of the American Civil Liberties Union—to talk about how to make the internet more secure. Their discussions continued onto online discussion boards, where cypherpunks chatted about how to extend the internet ideals of security and anonymity to money. By the time bitcoin launched in 2009, there was a homegrown community to support it and build businesses, including Coinbase. The cypherpunks are to Brian and Fred what the semiconductor pioneers were to Jobs. "I don't think Coinbase would have worked outside of Silicon Valley. It wasn't an accident I met Fred here or Charlie Lee at Google. I went to Silicon Valley because that's where the next generation of talent is," Brian says.

But for all Silicon Valley has to offer idealistic young inventors—culture, innovation, talent, and history—it still lacked one thing: deep reserves of capital and financial infrastructure required to bring inventions like bitcoin into the mainstream. The real seat of money for the United States—and for the world—remains where it has been for more than a century: Wall Street.

That half-mile of road in Lower Manhattan—famously described as a "street that begins with a graveyard and ends in a river"—and the blocks around it are home to a collection of skyscrapers that control the keys to trillions of dollars of investment capital: hedge funds, pension funds, private equity firms, family offices. Even in 2016, seven years after bitcoin launched, very little of that capital had flowed into the cryptocurrency economy.

Sure, crypto was flourishing in the contained community of advocates and believers, but Brian and others believed that a true breakout would arrive only when banks and other giant financial institutions took it seriously. These institutions were always on the hunt for new and exotic investments to juice their clients' portfolios. They put money in inventive hedging strategies, emerging market funds, and unusual commodity bets. If the Wall Street establishment could be persuaded to diversify its bets a little further and reallocate even 1 percent of that wealth into crypto, prices would go through the roof, vast reserves of capital would be invested in its growth, and the industry would soar.

Coinbase had made modest inroads. Since the launch of its GDAX exchange, professional traders had flocked to the platform to buy and sell bitcoin and Ethereum. These included wealthy day traders and, increasingly, a new species of hedge funders seeking the promise of high yields in the crypto markets. But these were at best knights and bishops on the chess board of finance, and Brian wanted the kings and queens of Wall Street. He decided to send an emissary to New York to force the issue.

* * *

Adam White had seen a lot of things in the Air Force and at Harvard Business School. And since joining Coinbase as employee number five, he had risen to run the GDAX exchange, which was turning into a cash machine for the company. He felt ready for a new challenge and figured he could handle anything the business world could throw at him. Brian threw Cantor Fitzgerald at him.

The famous firm embodied every stereotype of Wall Street's clubby culture. Working at Cantor Fitzgerald meant wearing suspenders and three-piece suits. It meant spending hours over expensive steak dinners and fine scotch, braying about how much money you made. Some of the firm's escapades read like sordid Hollywood plotlines. Its former London office was pilloried in an infamous 2008 *Spectator* magazine tell-all by a twenty-three-year-old female associate, who dished ugly details about Cantor's culture of unbridled boozing and skirt-chasing. The account describes her male colleagues calling her "Airbags" because of her breasts and guzzling £800 bottles of wine over lunch. A decade later, another woman in the firm's New York office would publicly blast the frat-boy culture she endured—including a boss who told her to "be respectful" when she complained of a colleague who shit in her Bernie Sanders coffee mug.

None of this, though, seemed to impair Cantor Fitzgerald's reputation as an A-list banking and brokerage firm for many of the world's wealthiest and most sophisticated companies. The Federal Reserve Bank of New York has designated it as one of a handful of firms to act as a market maker for federal securities, which means acting as Uncle Sam's bond broker.

And it was now Adam's job to sell Cantor Fitzgerald on the benefits of crypto and doing business with Coinbase, which would be a feather in the startup's cap and go a long way toward legitimizing an industry. He met reps from the firm on 59th Street in a tower overlooking Central Park. Cantor Fitzgerald's headquarters had long been located at the top of the World Trade Center's North Tower until a Boeing 767 jet struck the building five floors below them on September 11, 2001. The firm lost 658 employees—two-thirds of its New York workforce—including the brother of CEO Howard Lutnick. Defiantly, Lutnick brought the firm's trading markets back online the next week, saving the company and eventually paying out benefits to relatives of employees killed in the attack.

Now, Lutnick stood at the head of a phalanx of Cantor Fitzgerald staff who had come to meet Adam. Adam did not meet phalanx with phalanx. He brought the friendly, self-effacing, and easygoing disposition of a native Californian and little more. Lutnick quickly noticed Adam wore no tie and arrived with no retinue. And then he saw his business card: General Manager.

In Silicon Valley, titles—like clothes—are often informal, sometimes creative, like "Digital Prophet" or "Innovation Sherpa." Many startups treat titles like a rack of hoodies—pull one off the rack, try it on, try another. Find one you're comfortable with. Old-line finance firms, on the other hand, where high achievers earned nicknames like "Wolf of Wall Street" and "Human Piranha," treat titles as critical badges of power and status. Ranks like "executive managing director" and "senior managing director" matter. They send important signals about who is worth investing time in, who is serious, and who can be ignored. Lutnick scoffed at the idea that Coinbase would send a "general manager"—whatever that was—to waste his time. Didn't they know who he was?

"So I sat down with this big, sharp-elbowed financial company, trying to work a deal," Adam recalls. "There must have been a dozen of them and there was just me. Then the CEO laughs at me and goes, 'Hey, GM, are you going to make my coffee?' I came out to New York and got my ass handed to me by old-school traders."

Adam's mission had failed. Coinbase's campaign to crack the heart of Wall Street would have to wait another day. Meanwhile, other bankers were similarly dismissive of cryptocurrency. The most famous figure in American banking—JPMorgan Chase CEO Jamie Dimon—made clear what he thought of cryptocurrency, flatly telling the press that bitcoin would not survive.

But even as the lords of Wall Street sneered at cryptocurrency, not all their soldiers were so skeptical. At Coinbase, a growing pile of job applicants listed New York firms as their current employer. At Dimon's own firm, in a high-profile defection, senior executive Blythe Masters left to run a blockchain startup called Digital Asset. Masters was already renowned on Wall Street for inventing credit default swaps, the contracts Warren Buffett correctly labeled as "time bombs," which could (and did) set off a financial crisis. Now, she would become the face of a faction in the crypto world known as "blockchain, not bitcoin."

It was inevitable that as bitcoin grew, people without the same agenda as the libertarian types in the Valley would find useful apps for blockchain's ledger technology, and that's what was happening. "Blockchain, not bitcoin" meant you were part of the group that wanted to use the technology bitcoin had pioneered without the radical decentralized system that let anyone in the world be part of it—a members-only system that produced a tamper-proof common ledger similar to the bitcoin one. For banks and big companies, "blockchain, not bitcoin" promised all of the innovative parts of Satoshi Nakamoto's creation minus the controversy, amateurish oversight, and sketchy figures.

In addition to Digital Asset, a group of former bankers with a penchant for fine suits and first-class airfare launched R3, a consortium of dozens of banks, including Goldman Sachs and JP Morgan who declared bitcoin irrelevant and said their blockchain software, which was closed and proprietary—unlike bitcoin—would supersede it. IBM, meanwhile, built a blockchain used by shipping firms to track cargo and by food producers to track pork and lettuce shipments.

For the bitcoin believers and advocates, this was heretical, and dubious—like punk rockers observing a record label trying to co-opt and re-create their culture for profit. Not only did it go against their core beliefs, they knew it wouldn't work.

"I was always railing against it because it was complete bullshit," says Fred. Critics alleged "blockchain, not bitcoin" was a marketing stunt and that the underlying product amounted to no more than a glorified database shared among friends. The benefit of hindsight suggests they were right. In less than two years, the big-name banks that had signed on to R3's grand consortium project had all pulled out, and interest in its proprietary blockchain has shriveled. Masters's Digital Asset hasn't fared any better, and Masters herself resigned with little to show for the once-vaunted project that had attracted more than $100 million from investors. On Wall Street, it would become clear by 2017 that "blockchain, not bitcoin" was a flop. The phrase died a quiet death.

Even if the "blockchain, not bitcoin" experiments fizzled, they still served as a stepping-stone for a growing number of people in the traditional finance world to discover crypto. It demystified the tech. And a few firms like Circle and the Winklevoss twins' Gemini, which *did* trade in bitcoin right there in New York, made the case that Coinbase and other Silicon Valley firms would have no monopoly on the emerging industry. Circle, Gemini, and a handful of other firms were real crypto players but with some East Coast flavor. They did not engage in antics like pajamas at work or all-night hackathons but still lured hundreds of traders and engineers away from traditional Wall Street jobs.

For those migrating to crypto, the appeal of ditching Wall Street was about something more than just money—even as the price of bitcoin and Ethereum kept climbing. It was about lifestyle. Like bitcoin itself, a career in crypto promised an escape from authority and the buttoned-up banking world.

Jeff Dorman, a broad-shouldered trader with intense eyes and receding hair, remembers his days grinding it out in the trading trenches of Lehman Brothers and Merrill Lynch before he joined the crypto asset management firm Arca. "I came up in this *Full Metal Jacket* kind of environment," he says, referencing Stanley Kubrik's brutal depiction of

Marine Corp boot camp in the Vietnam War era. "All the things you read about investment banking are true. I'd stay up till 3 in the morning to make sure a PowerPoint was perfect—as if it was so important that the outcome of a deal would come down to a typo in a PowerPoint slide."

The crypto business, by contrast, meant less rigor and fewer rules. As crypto tech seeped into finance, so did its culture. East Coast firms weren't going full Valley culture, but the Valley's DNA was in the firms. "When you're trading in the traditional industry five days a week, you have all these things you have to finish before market close," says Dorman. "The 24/7 nature of crypto means a different pace. You have to train yourself to chill out."

Likewise, finance culture was seeping into cryptocurrency. As the price of bitcoin and Ethereum soared in 2016, more traders began to see cryptocurrencies as a commodity just like wheat or oil or sugar. This, in turn, set off a clamor of activity in Chicago—home to the country's commodities markets—as firms rushed to design futures and options contracts that would let traders bet on price swings. And the action wasn't just in bitcoin and Ethereum. On loosely regulated overseas exchanges, traders speculated on a galaxy of other cryptocurrencies that began to double and triple in price. Litecoin fans, for instance, likened the currency to bitcoin's little brother and pointed out that its network had been up and running before Ethereum's. XRP was a versatile currency launched by the founder of the infamous Mt. Gox exchange, and the company supporting it, Ripple, had evolved into a full-blown financial firm that pitched XRP to banks as a way to move money across borders. Other currencies offered no rhyme or reason for their existence or even any assurance they could not be hacked or manipulated by unscrupulous insiders. For many traders, it didn't matter. A bull market was barreling forward as the price of every type of cryptocurrency kept climbing.

Business schools took notice, finally. Only a few years earlier, Coinbase's Adam White had pleaded with his professors at Harvard Business School to allow him to write about bitcoin. The school had refused. Now, impatient students formed crypto clubs on their own. Harvard and other top MBA programs began to introduce courses in blockchain and bitcoin, prepping the pipeline to the upper echelons of banks and corporate America for careers in cryptocurrency.

At Cornell University, computer science professor Emin Gün Sirer helped found the Initiative for Cryptocurrencies and Contracts, a sort of crypto think tank with partner schools in Berkeley, London, and Switzerland. Stanford Law School announced its first class in cryptocurrency and cybercrime. Its professor? None other than Katie Haun, who four years earlier had been asked to prosecute bitcoin and was now one of the country's leading crypto authorities.

The media's coverage of crypto also started to go mainstream. While the tech press reported on Bitcoin, financial media mostly ignored it—save for the occasional headline that dismissed it altogether, as when the *Washington Post* warned in late 2014, "Bitcoin's Financial Network Is Doomed," or Yahoo Finance declared the same year "This Could be the End of the Bitcoin Era." By 2016, outlets like *Bloomberg* and the *Wall Street Journal* assigned business reporters to cover crypto. Books like *The Age of Cryptocurrency* and *Blockchain Revolution* further increased the ledger technology's credibility.

The transformation wasn't instant. Bitcoin's outlaw origins kept poking through. Hedge funds and universities were exploring the promise of bitcoin, sure, but the reality was that Satoshi's currency continued to provide the best anonymous marketplace for extortion schemes and drug sales. Silk Road had been shut down, but a new online bazaar called AlphaBay sprung up on the dark web to take its place as a clearinghouse for criminal activity. And it let customers pay with bitcoin and a new species of cryptocurrency called Monero, which was designed specifically to scramble the record of transactions in a way that made it extremely difficult to connect transactions to any individual's account—making it ideal to thwart law enforcement.

The other longtime strike against crypto—besides popularity with criminals—was that it could be hacked, and that was still true. In August of 2016 thieves broke into one of the world's largest exchanges, a shadowy Hong Kong outfit called Bitfinex, and stole more than $73 million worth of customers' bitcoins. The exchange responded by imposing a 36 percent haircut on all of its clients—literally confiscating more than a third of their money to make up for the loss. The Bitfinex debacle was the biggest hack since Mt. Gox and caused the price of bitcoin to tumble, briefly.

At Coinbase, Brian was not fazed by the Bitfinex hack. He knew that it represented an opportunity. He saw more and more people starting to embrace crypto, and he sensed crypto was about to get bigger. Much bigger.

9

Brian Has a Master Plan

B rian breathed a sigh of satisfaction as he clicked on "publish" and his blog post went live. It was September of 2016, a month after the Bitfinex hack, and he was wearing a plain black T-shirt. Like other Silicon Valley CEOs, he had taken on a distinct sartorial style as a type of self-branding. Brian's style wasn't as conspicuous as Mark Zuckerberg's hoodie or Steve Jobs's turtleneck—an affect later copied by Twitter CEO Jack Dorsey and disgraced Theranos founder Elizabeth Holmes. Instead, Brian took to donning a simple T-shirt—usually black, sometimes white—for speeches and public appearances. It was a nod to simplicity and focus.

Since founding Coinbase, Brian had kept his blog as a chronicle of product announcements, hiring milestones, and other signs of progress. This blog post was different. It was broader and more ambitious. Unsubtly titled "The Coinbase Secret Master Plan," it set out Brian's sweeping vision for the future of cryptocurrency.

Crypto was like the internet, he explained and, like the internet, it would have a four-step development. The initial two steps, which would bring crypto to one million and then to ten million people, were well under way. The first had been the creation of new blockchain protocols like bitcoin and Ethereum to create and distribute money. Next came services to trade and store crypto. The third phase in crypto's development, Brian said, would be software allowing people to interact more directly with blockchain technology—the equivalent of how the arrival of browsers like Netscape and Explorer let anybody discover the internet. The fourth and final step, Brian predicted, would come in the form of blockchain apps that let people do things like borrow, lend, and invest without relying on a bank. Step four, he wrote, would mark the inauguration of Finance 2.0 and bring one billion people into the emerging crypto universe. If this was the future, then Coinbase's master plan was to lay stepping-stones to Finance 2.0 while investing in other companies doing the same.

The prose in the blog reflected Brian—both technocratic and visionary. "At Coinbase we are passionate about creating an open financial system for the world. By open we mean not controlled by any one country or company (just like the internet). We think this is the highest leverage way to bring about more economic freedom, innovation, efficiency, and equality of opportunity in the world," he wrote.

The master plan made perfect sense to Brian, even if it didn't make *any* sense to most people, including many in the traditional financial world. Crypto had made inroads into a few corners of Wall Street and could be traded along with other commodities, but the idea of a billion people using crypto seemed far-fetched to everyone who hadn't been steeped in bitcoin for years. But in true Silicon Valley fashion, Brian thought it best to think big, and he had Coinbase's board behind him. However, first he would have to inspire Coinbase's own employees.

Giant and far-flung business visions are usually associated with Valley and tech CEOs who have outsize personalities. Steve Jobs is the archetype. Even as the late Apple CEO introduced some of the most profoundly disruptive technology the world has ever seen, he nourished a cult of personality with his distinct appearance and a stage presence worthy of P. T. Barnum. Elon Musk, who runs both the electric car company Tesla and the rocket maker SpaceX, likes to share extravagant plans for living on Mars and building high-speed tunnels between US cities. In person and online, Musk is combative and outrageous—picking fights with the SEC on Twitter and smoking weed during live radio interviews. At least part of this is a calculated attempt to build up the Musk mystique. Amazon's Jeff Bezos envisions people living in space colonies.

Being of the Valley, it would not be unusual for Brian to think big and think big publicly. But Brian was nothing like Jobs or Musk or Bezos. He was a self-described introvert CEO. Every early Coinbase employee describes Brian as "awkward." Several point, in particular, to his first attempt at delivering an inspirational speech during a company retreat in Napa Valley—summing it up as "painful" and "oh my God." One employee said, "The joke was always that he's on the [autism] spectrum somewhere," before adding thoughtfully, "but with Silicon Valley, fuck, I think 80 percent of the founders here are a little bit odd when it comes to social skills."

Brian had enough self-awareness to try and learn. That wasn't difficult. Since he was a teenager, he had been possessed by a pathological desire for self-improvement. If there was something he didn't understand, he read about it until he did. If he met someone who knew more than he did, he asked them questions. One time, upon receiving a performance evaluation from an outside consultant, he emailed it to everyone at Coinbase, asking them to weigh in, too. For Brian, leading was just another skill he would have to learn.

At the urging of Coinbase's board, Brian and Fred had invested heavily in Silicon Valley's best coaches, and these efforts began to show results, albeit with early hiccups like the infatuation with Conscious Leadership. The coaches sanded off some of the rough edges that had led *Bloomberg Businessweek* to describe the pair as humorless "Vulcan bankers." The work of office manager Nathalie McGrath to build a more human office culture, with costume events and karaoke nights, had also helped make Brian more approachable.

Nevertheless, Brian not only acknowledged he was an introvert, but came to embrace it. Like Jobs or Musk or Bezos, Brian had a sweeping vision—bring crypto to one billion people and disrupt the multi-trillion-dollar finance industry. Unlike them, he couldn't try to carry out that vision through sheer force of personality. "I didn't really know exactly what a CEO was," he says. "I thought maybe you had to be a military general, like barking orders to people. You shouldn't try to be something you're not. Being fake is the worst kind of leadership."

Brian had learned another lesson: being introverted wasn't the same as being weak. Since the beginning, he had fought time and again to exert total control over Coinbase, whether this meant nudging out his Y Combinator partner or dictating terms to the startup's angel investors. And as Coinbase grew bigger, he turned to a new tactic to ensure he would keep that control.

In Silicon Valley, executives like Mark Zuckerberg have discovered a way to ensure they are not just chief executives, but kings of the companies they found. Google's founders, Larry Page and Sergey Brin, used the same trick to stay in control, even as they distributed more and more of the company's stock. The secret for staying in power involved creating a new class of shares with super voting rights. Ordinarily, one share of a company's stock comes with an equivalent degree of voting power. If the company in question has created one hundred shares, the owner holding 1 percent of the firm's assets gets one vote out of a hundred. Super voting shares bust the math: an individual who owns such stock might get ten votes for every share, ensuring that he or she can outvote ordinary investors who own a much bigger proportion of the company. In a variation of the scheme, a company might issue new shares with no voting power at all, thus increasing the power of extant voting shares. This lets some investors partake in the company's fortune but with no say in how it's run. No matter the specifics, the outcome is the same: founders obtain a hammerlock on critical issues such as board composition, product strategy, or anything else that affects the direction of the company.

This is what Brian did as Coinbase grew. As the company raised a $75 million Series C and then a $100 million Series D investment round—key milestones on the path to taking a company public—it handed out millions of new shares, but also created a new class of shares for Brian that would guarantee he could outvote those investors and anyone else. Like Zuckerberg and the Google founders, Brian had an iron grip on Coinbase for now and for the foreseeable future. By the time he posted his visionary blog post, Brian had the power he needed and was learning to lead a company that was growing faster than he anticipated.

．　．　．

A key test of Brian's leadership came as competition to lure professional traders heated up. While Coinbase's bread and butter had always been retail investors and hobbyists, its professional exchange, GDAX, had set out to capture the market for wealthy traders—called "whales"—and the growing number of hedge funds and other Wall Street players dipping their toes into the crypto world.

An early version of GDAX launched in 2015 and, after it added Ethereum, the exchange took off. To track its progress, Coinbase placed giant monitors around the office showing GDAX's market share compared with other exchanges. The company was not number one. That distinction belonged to Bitfinex, the Hong Kong–based exchange that had endured a series of hacking scandals—including the one in 2016 that saw it lose $72 million in bitcoin to thieves and then impose a 36 percent haircut on of all its customers' holdings to make up for the loss. Despite its general sketchiness—no one was quite sure who controlled it—Bitfinex still enjoyed a global base of customers who liked its fast-and-loose approach to financial regulation, which allowed them to get richer quicker. Coinbase couldn't—wouldn't—compete with that. Since the beginning, the company had tried to do right by regulators and, on GDAX, it catered to customers who cared about compliance. Targeting compliance-conscious Americans and traders in other countries with tight banking laws, GDAX began to build market share and soon pushed past a San Francisco rival, Kraken. But then the graphs on the giant office monitors started to move in the wrong direction—down.

GDAX's growth stagnated in mid-2016, surrendering some of its market share to rivals like Bitfinex and other renegade exchanges, which had wooed customers with low prices and more types of crypto to trade.

More crucially, Coinbase and GDAX had a new and serious competitor: the Winklevoss twins.

Cameron and Tyler Winklevoss first gained fame via Aaron Sorkin's acclaimed 2010 film *The Social Network*, which focuses on betrayal and intrigue surrounding the founding of Facebook. The movie depicts the twins, played by Armie Hammer, as jocks outwitted by a scheming Mark Zuckerberg, who dubs them "the Winklevii." While the film painted Zuckerberg as unsympathetic, it also left a lasting impression of the Winklevoss twins as lummoxes—an impression they did little to dispel by trading on their movie fame to appear in a moronic pistachio commercial that took a shot at Zuckerberg.

In reality, the twins are little like their popular caricatures. While their physical stature is striking—as Cameron's character snarls in the movie, "I'm six-foot-five, 220, and there's two of me"—their accomplishments go beyond their rowing careers at Harvard and the Beijing Olympics. Far from being silver-spoon brats, the twins were hardworking students who, while still in high school, translated Latin works of St. Augustine and other early scholars with their father. In person, they are different from each other—Cameron is more serious and hard-charging while Tyler is more jovial—but both are thoughtful and well-spoken. One thing *The Social Network* did get right, though, is their driving ambition.

In the battle over Facebook, the twins won a settlement after their lawyers obtained a series of damning messages from Zuckerberg—including one where he gloated how he would "fuck them . . . probably in the ear." Notwithstanding the ear-fucking, Cameron and Tyler made out very well, obtaining a $65 million payout in 2008, the bulk of which they took in Facebook stock. That ballooned to over $500 million a few years later. Around this time, they struck gold again. As their biographer Ben Mezrich writes of their decision to take the Zuckerberg payout in stock, "For the [allegedly] foolish, batshit-crazy twins, this proved to be one of the greatest business decisions of all time—topped only, perhaps, by their choice to invest $11 million of that settlement in bitcoin in 2013."

Cameron and Tyler's next business decision—to back the dissolute Charlie Shrem and his BitInstant project—was less auspicious.

BitInstant, which offered bitcoin buying and merchant services, got crushed by Coinbase, and Shrem went to jail for breaking money-laundering laws. The twins, though, rebounded. They sought a rematch with Coinbase with the launch of Gemini, their squeaky-clean exchange aimed at professional traders. And in the early rounds of this fight, they won decisively.

"Gemini came out of stealth [in late 2015] and we watched them on the office monitors creep up every week and then surpass us," recalls Adam White, who led Coinbase's pro trading exchange GDAX. This was a double blow. Not only was Coinbase's new cash machine faltering but it was losing to a competitor that likewise styled itself as a "white knight of crypto"—a place for compliance-minded investors who needed an exchange that stayed on the right side of regulators. The flagging exchange situation was a crisis that needed leadership. Brian stepped in.

In an urgent email, he summoned Adam White, other GDAX executives, and other key people from across Coinbase—from legal, from marketing, and from design. "Fix this," he told them at a tense lunch, "and fix it now." The Brian who appeared at the lunch was unlike the leader his staff had seen before—direct and authoritative. Barking orders like a general may not have been his style but, on this occasion, Brian mustered a military-style persona, directing the different silos of Coinbase to work together like never before.

"Winning the exchange space is fundamental; it's foundational," he said. What he meant was that if Coinbase couldn't hold its own against the likes of Gemini, they could forget about the rest of Brian's master plan.

The all-hands intervention worked. Services like GDAX are, at the end of the day, products, and products don't succeed if they don't have support from the nonproduct people in a company. By shoving the exchange to the top of everyone's agenda at Coinbase, Brian brought the exchange back from disaster. The graphs on the office monitors took on their old appearance as GDAX regained market share, while Gemini shriveled. For the second time in three years, the Winklevoss twins lost to Coinbase.

● ● ●

By 2017, Coinbase had grown to hundreds of employees, and Brian was learning to lead them all. He was still an introvert but no longer one who retreated into the private world of his headphones for twelve hours at a time. But even with dozens of direct reports, and less self-imposed seclusion, Brian grew lonelier in the role.

The departure of Olaf, Brian's good friend, was followed by others. Charlie Lee, the company's fifth employee, had a new home and a family who had grown tired of his long hours at Coinbase. Charlie also owned a hoard of Litecoin. He had created the lighter version of bitcoin while at Google in 2011, and the digital currency had since become worth billions, its value trailing only bitcoin and Ethereum. Litecoin's value would soar still further, Charlie suspected, if more people could buy it. And the best way to make that happen would be to sell it on Coinbase.

A popular story in crypto circles tells of Charlie secretly building Litecoin capacity into Coinbase's code and, late one night, pushing the code live with no warning, only to be fired the next day. It's a good story, but it's not true. A programming feat like adding Litecoin support to Coinbase would take a much longer time to build and numerous hours to launch. It can't be done overnight. Also, Coinbase uses what employees call an "eye of Sauron" to ensure no one can unilaterally mess with its code without tripping alarms.

Coinbase did launch Litecoin in the spring of 2017—with Brian's full approval—and the price shot up 25 percent. The press pronounced the bounce was due to the "Coinbase effect," a term that would create publicity, and trouble, for the company in the future. Two months later, Charlie announced he was leaving Coinbase.

. . .

Charlie's departure meant the loss of another longtime and trusted employee, but a much bigger blow for Brian had come months earlier. Fred had left.

Since his epic rant that pushed Coinbase to adopt Ethereum, Fred had grown restless. He was cofounder of the company, but Brian was in charge. While the pair had found an equilibrium early on—Brian ran product, and Fred took care of the business side—Coinbase could no longer contain both their ambitions. Fred wanted to call all the shots, but that wasn't going to happen at Coinbase. Sensing the beginnings of an unprecedented bull run for crypto, he decided to strike out on his own to build apps and launch a hedge fund. "I enjoyed being a spirit leader at Coinbase," he recalls, adding that since leaving, he and Brian have become better friends than ever.

The formal goodbye came during a Friday morning meeting in front of all the employees, many of whom were shaken by the news. Fred spoke reverently of his time at Coinbase and his optimism about the future of cryptocurrency. "What I wanted most was for the company to do well. I had hired everyone who was there. It's like leaving your family in a way," he recalls.

And then the tough and unsentimental money man—the one who had exhorted the company to charge through brick walls—did something he hadn't done in many years. He started to cry.

Brian had published his "Secret Master Plan" in September of 2016. But as his ambitions swelled, the following months placed more on his shoulders than ever before, and he now had few trusted friends to help. And as the beginnings of an impending crypto mania began to swirl, Coinbase began to face a new set of problems. Not least of which was the US government.

10

Uncle Sam Comes Calling

On November 9, 2016, Washington, DC, woke to gloomy rain and the news that a political outsider, Donald J. Trump, would be the next president of the United States. Financial markets shuddered; futures contracts for major stock indexes traded 5 percent lower, and the price of oil fell. Gold, traditionally a haven in times of turbulence, ticked up. So did bitcoin, which rose 3 percent on news of Trump's election. For bitcoin boosters, that small price jump would be the only good news about cryptocurrency to come out of Washington for the next three years.

On the other side of the country, David Utzke, a decorated special forces veteran based in California, was creating trouble for bitcoin. After serving overseas with the US Army and Navy, Utzke had sought a new way to serve his country when he got home. He found it with another fearsome organization: the Internal Revenue Service. Now forty-something, with perfect teeth and rigid posture, Utzke was scouring the globe for tax cheats.

Many people regard the IRS as an agency of gnomish bean counters who spend all day hunkered over tax returns. Fewer know that the agency also outfits a formidable law enforcement division that employs people like Utzke—accountants with badges and guns—who train at the same school as agents from the FBI and the DEA.

The IRS was one of the agencies that had quickly grasped the criminal potential of cryptocurrency. One of its special agents, Gary Alford, helped break open the federal investigation into the Silk Road crime bazaar. Alford has a strange habit—he always reads documents three times—but this idiosyncrasy paid off when, on one of his triple readings, he recognized a connection between a Gmail address and the Dread Pirate Roberts, the anonymous mastermind of the Silk Road. Alford's discovery led the Justice Department to identify and convict Ross Ulbricht, aka the Dread Pirate.

Alford's colleague Utzke had foreseen the rise of digital money way back in the 1980s and chose a novel concentration of studies in college—economics, forensic accounting, and computer science—in anticipation of something like bitcoin arriving one day. At the IRS, as the crypto markets picked up steam in early 2016, he embarked on an investigation of crypto tax evasion. This entailed an electronic search of all IRS returns between 2013 and 2015 to determine how many included a Form 8949—used to declare capital gains. Utzke then filtered those millions of filings to identify anyone who reported "property likely related to bitcoin." He found only 802 such filings. That was the number of Americans who had reported gains or losses related to bitcoin the previous year.

That word *property* was key. In 2014, the IRS issued a statement designating cryptocurrencies like bitcoin as property, not currency. Owning bitcoin was just like owning a house or shares of Apple stock. If the price went up and the owner sold her shares, she would pay Uncle

Sam under capital gains rules—typically about 10 percent of the profit. If the owner held onto the property for less than a year before selling it, it would be classified as a short-term gain and the resulting tax would be higher. Bitcoin's legal status as property also meant that using it to buy anything, even a cup of coffee, could trigger a tax obligation. For someone like Olaf, who lived on bitcoin for several years, a strict interpretation of the IRS rules would result in an unending tax nightmare.

Utzke looked at his findings again. That number, 802, was shockingly small given that millions of US citizens reportedly owned bitcoin wallets and, according to his calculations, there had been over $10 billion in bitcoin transactions in 2015 alone. The more he looked into who was using bitcoin, the more sure he was that digital currency was a vector for tax evasion.

Utzke decided to squeeze a tax cheat who was already facing criminal charges to tell him more about bitcoin. This person had evaded taxes by using shell companies to funnel money into foreign brokerage accounts, and then back to the United States via withdrawals at ATMs. The tax dodger told Utzke this scheme had become a bother and that he found bitcoin provided an easier way to duck the IRS. Instead of sloshing money through different companies and accounts, he converted the cash into bitcoin, then bought cars, boats, and other items he could flip for dollars.

Utzke also discovered other bitcoin buyers who used less blatant but equally illegal ways to cheat. These included two companies whose accounts treated bitcoin purchases as technology expenses so as to classify them as tax deductions—the equivalent of trying to write off the purchase of gold bars or Euro notes as a business expense. When confronted, these two companies would be in for a world of hurt. And so would Coinbase. Utzke discovered, unsurprisingly, that the two organizations had bought their bitcoin through Coinbase.

Coinbase, unlike most bitcoin sellers, had something the IRS wanted very much and few others in the bitcoin world had: a detailed profile of every one of its customers, including their name, home address, date of birth, and much more. These records would make it easy for the IRS to compare a list of Coinbase customers who had sold bitcoin against the agency's own records to see who had failed to pay taxes.

From the outset, Brian had set out to make Coinbase the law-abiding good guy amid an industry rife with scams and scoundrels. Board member Chris Dixon had even taken to calling Coinbase "the white knight of crypto." Now, ironically, the white knight's decision to comply with "know your customer" laws had made it easy pickings for the IRS's first major investigation into cryptocurrency—even as the more renegade exchanges, which operated in secrecy and skirted banking laws, avoided scrutiny.

Utzke's investigation produced a subpoena that landed at Coinbase in late 2016 like a grenade. Company lawyers showed it to Fred shortly before he left Coinbase. Normally unflappable, Fred groaned, "Oh shit, this is serious." There was no running through a brick wall built by the IRS. They brought the letter to Brian.

The subpoena was a nightmare they'd have had a hard time imagining but for the fact they were looking right at it. The IRS wasn't after the account information of a few tax cheats it had been tracking. It wanted the identity of *every* Coinbase customer who had sold bitcoin—more than five hundred thousand of them—and every attendant piece of personally identifying information about them, including any email they might have sent to Coinbase as well as all power of attorney letters they executed with Coinbase. This was shaping up to be the Spanish Inquisition of tax investigations.

The subpoena meant hell two times over for Coinbase. First, the burden of rounding up and printing the details of *half a million* customer records to send to the IRS would require Coinbase staff to burn hundreds—possibly thousands—of hours on paperwork rather than building out the company's crypto services.

The second hell was the reputational scorching Coinbase would likely have to endure. From the start, Coinbase's notion of centralizing keys and accounts had been problematic for the bitcoin purists, who viewed the tech as antiestablishment, anonymous, and a way to break power structures. Many of them had blamed Coinbase for betraying bitcoin's libertarian values. Those values called on individuals to trust no central authority and rely instead on cryptographic private keys to guard their stashes. Their knock on Coinbase came in the form of a taunt—"not your keys, not your coins"—a dig at the company's practice of storing its customers' bitcoin for them. Now, if the government scooped up five hundred thousand Coinbase customer accounts, it would prove the critics right. Coinbase would be despised for selling out its users' privacy. Given the vitriol, including death threats, hurled at the company during the block-size debates, it was hard to fathom how Coinbase would come through this.

Faced with crushing heaps of paperwork and a PR catastrophe, Brian did the only thing he thought he could do. He said no to the IRS. In a blog post, Brian said the likes of Citibank or PayPal or Charles Schwab would never go along with such a request from the IRS—and there was no way Coinbase would either. Bracing for millions in legal bills, the company filed to quash the subpoena as illegal and invasive.

"Asking for detailed transaction information on so many people, simply for using digital currency, is a violation of their privacy, and is not the best way for us to accomplish our mutual objective," Brian wrote.

A two-year legal battle yielded some wins. Coinbase persuaded a judge to winnow down—though not quash—the subpoena. In the end, the IRS won the right to obtain limited records on more than thirteen thousand of Coinbase's biggest customers—those who had done over $20,000 in business or conducted more than two hundred transactions in a year. Coinbase also provided 1099-K forms to large customers, a practice that mirrored what brokerages like Fidelity have long done. Neither Coinbase nor its customers were particularly happy with this outcome, but there was a silver lining: the legal fight would help bring Coinbase and other crypto companies closer to the world of mainstream financial institutions.

· · ·

While the IRS had declared bitcoin was property, officials at the SEC were deliberating over whether it was technically a security, a tradeable financial asset. Meanwhile, at the Treasury Department, the Financial Crimes Enforcement Network treated it as a currency. And yet another agency, the CFTC (Commodity Futures Trading Commission), said bitcoin was a commodity, which would mean it was a good or a service. These technicalities could be mind-numbing, but they also meant a legal minefield for the emerging crypto industry.

Ironically, in the course of trying to classify and put checks on bitcoin, the US government also become one of the biggest owners of it. As a result of the Silk Road takedown, the FBI had seized around 150,000 bitcoin from the site's mastermind and then sold them off for millions of dollars in a series of auctions run by the US Marshals Service. Meanwhile, the Bureau of Alcohol, Tobacco, Firearms and Explosives, the Drug Enforcement Agency, the Secret Service, and others began confiscating crypto in the course of their investigations. Some of the bitcoin ended up in the hands of the Marshals, while other stashes simply went missing. The US government couldn't keep track of its own bitcoin—even as it was creating a regulatory ordeal for everyone else who touched the currency.

And that was just the feds. State regulators wanted a say too. The New York Department of Financial Services, jealously guarding its role as watchdog of Wall Street, dumped another load of paperwork on the crypto sector in the form of licensure. Any company that wanted to deal crypto in the Empire State would have to obtain a so-called Bit License—a process that cost over $100,000 and could take years to complete. This bureaucratic hellhole stank of revolving-door politics. The powerful official who created the license, Benjamin Lawsky, soon quit the Department of Financial Services and created a consultancy that specialized in—what else?—helping firms navigate crypto regulation. For bitcoin ideologues, Lawsky's stunt simply reaffirmed their belief about the tyrannical nature of government. "New York is that abusive, controlling ex you broke up with three years ago, but they keep stalking you," snarled Jesse Powell, the libertarian CEO of the Kraken exchange.

Another influential figure in bitcoin, Erik Voorhees, was even less impressed. Voorhees had developed one of the first bitcoin applications, a gambling game called Satoshi Dice, and ran a company called ShapeShift that let customers exchange one type of crypto for another. Even by libertarian standards, Voorhees was a radical. His political passions included the Free State movement, a campaign to persuade tens of thousands of people to move to New Hampshire. Their influx into that low-population state, the Free Staters hoped, would allow them to create a stronghold for antigovernment zealots. Many in the movement also promoted bitcoin as a way to subvert the state's control over the money supply. Voorhees watched what was unfolding in New York with dismay. "Bit License is officially law in New York today," he tweeted. "Shed a tear for freedom, capitalism and innovation. Then comply, citizen."

Not everyone in crypto circles shared Voorhees's views, of course. Many others, including Brian, hoped thoughtful, careful regulation could bring stability to the crypto markets and help it become even more mainstream.

Unfortunately, the emerging US regulatory regime for cryptocurrency was not providing stability, but instead wrapping it in red tape. Multiple agencies were still arguing over whether this stuff was money or property or a commodity like frozen orange juice. Rules began to multiply from state to state. Navigating the knots of red tape was making markets less stable and slowing crypto's legitimacy.

Meanwhile, other countries were carving out safe harbors from the US regulatory storms where crypto firms could operate under relative calm. The state of Zug in Switzerland, for instance, created a "Crypto Valley" where firms could experiment with new business models without stepping into a regulatory bear trap. American entrepreneurs and investors began to warn that a generation of crypto innovation could decamp to foreign shores if the United States didn't dispel its regulatory haze.

Blame could not be put entirely at the feet of the regulators. The IRS and other agencies were simply using the tools they had—and nearly all those tools had been created before bitcoin existed. The regulators were trying to stuff crypto, a new technology, into old legal boxes designed for an earlier era of finance. The situation wasn't much different from when cars began appearing on American roads. Lacking laws to regulate automobiles, governments in the early twentieth century did their best by adapting rules designed for horses and carriages. In the long run, of course, this proved impractical, and new laws were required to regulate cars.

Coinbase has many of the same backers as Airbnb, Uber, and other Silicon Valley companies that built their business on what some call "regulatory arbitrage"—exploiting regulatory loopholes while also unleashing feel-good PR that includes fluffy phrases like "the sharing economy." The strategy had worked well for those other startups, letting them grow big enough to fight every court battle and curry favor with politicians. But Brian knew that for the crypto industry to catch a break, it would need new laws. And that meant going to Congress to help lawmakers make good ones. It was time for Brian to go to Washington.

· · ·

While Wall Street and the Valley are very different places—as Adam White found out when he met with Cantor Fitzgerald—they do share a zest for free markets and cosmopolitan culture that makes them oddball distant cousins. The Valley and Washington, on the other hand, are about as closely related as a hamster to a hippopotamus. Most people in the Capitol regard the Valley with hostility and suspicion, while most California tech geeks possess a nearly physical aversion to the politics and lobbying that permeate DC (though tech giants like Google and Facebook eventually become adept at the lobbying game themselves).

The Coinbase crew had already made several forays into Washington over the years in an effort to win over lawmakers to the potential of crypto. What they encountered did little to improve their opinion. Juan Suarez, the company's longtime lawyer, had tried and failed to educate lawmakers about cryptocurrency. "I tried to explain bitcoin to people in DC, but all they would do was ask about Olaf's eccentric blog posts from three years earlier," he said, referring to rambling essays written by his former colleague.

Brian had little time for DC-style politics. What was the point of engaging with pols when, in his view, he could use Coinbase to bring economic freedom to a billion people? One exception, however, was his hometown congresswoman, the powerful Speaker of the House and Democratic leader Nancy Pelosi. During a meeting in her San Francisco office, she did not raise her liberal priorities, but instead piled on the charm, telling Brian how much she respected and admired entrepreneurs. Brian could handle someone like Pelosi on Coinbase's home turf on the West Coast. It was the city of Washington, DC—populated with partisans inflamed by narrow issues and often ignorant of tech—he could do without.

Regardless of Brian's ease with Pelosi, the IRS investigation and the gathering regulatory storm meant Coinbase had to double down on its political efforts. Brian hired Mike Lempres, a political fixer who had served as associate attorney general of the Justice Department in the 1990s and had worked with President Donald Trump's future Attorney General William Barr as well as Robert Mueller, who would lead a high-profile investigation into Russian interference in American elections. A fifth-generation son of San Francisco, Lempres has a fluff of white hair around a growing bald spot, but he still projects youth and vigor. At Coinbase, he drew a tough assignment: sell Brian on Washington, DC. After all, if the company wanted to notch a political win for cryptocurrency, sending its CEO as an emissary could be key to its strategy. "I told him, 'Brian, I hope you like it.' I want you to be here at least twice a year," said Lempres, adding ruefully, "he didn't like it."

Their joint visit stirred little in Brian besides a strong urge to go back to California. The city's heat and humidity were oppressive. The DC schmoozing culture annoyed him. He liked people who built things rather than just bloviated about them. This included the US senators he met. One of them, a stalwart of the Democrats, he declared to his Coinbase colleagues, was a "complete and total ass."

About the only thing he liked about DC was the underground train that whisks members of Congress between different places on Capitol Hill. Other than that, the trip was a bust. Lempres's hopes of imparting to Brian the ways of Washington went nowhere. On their way back, Lempres recalls, "Brian wanted to solve the whole problem with the SEC on our return flight. He thought it was time to go back to first principles and rethink the whole agency. The thing is that there's a hundred years of SEC law out there, and they're not about to change it for him."

With or without Brian, policy would be made. Slowly, glacially, Washington grappled with cryptocurrency, lumbering toward a plan. Meanwhile, the thriving world of crypto investors was not going to wait for the feds. As Congress dithered, one of the most outrageous financial bubbles in modern history was swelling faster than a new celebrity's ego.

11

Initial Coin Insanity

On June 25, 2017, news raced around social media that Ethereum creator Vitalik Buterin had died in a car crash. Speculators panicked. Prices fell 20 percent, lopping $4 billion off Ethereum's value in hours.

The next day, a tweet from Vitalik himself went viral. The tweet showed a photo of him, very much alive, holding up a piece of paper with the number of a newly mined block in the Ethereum blockchain and a figure, known as a hash, that had just unlocked the block. Vitalik's tweet was the blockchain equivalent of a hostage holding up a daily newspaper as proof that he was alive. The picture proved Vitalik was not dead. The price of Ethereum bounced back up.

The car wreck story was a hoax perpetrated by trolls on the website 4chan, either to manipulate the market or simply to pull off a ghoulish prank. Either way, the stunt demonstrated how critical Vitalik—the strange, spectral genius who had created Ethereum— was to the currency's success and the success of crypto in general.

It also underscored how Ethereum had taken center stage, over bitcoin, in the 2017 crypto boom.

Early in the year, the price of Ethereum was $13. By summer, its value had increased thirtyfold and was nudging $400. And the big run-up was just beginning. Meanwhile, thanks in large part to Ethereum, dozens and then hundreds of other cryptocurrencies began to take off.

. . .

Ethereum, you may recall, was Vitalik's smart contract machine that had emerged as bitcoin's main rival in the blockchain world. But it also served as the most popular platform for building other cryptocurrency projects. Suppose someone wanted to offer file storage or sports betting on a blockchain? One option would be to build a blockchain specifically for that purpose. A much easier option, though, would be to use smart contracts to build that service on top of Ethereum. In the emerging crypto industry, Ethereum was like a new type of internet, and these new third-party projects—like file sharing or sports betting—were the websites that ran on top of it.

Ethereum is different than the internet in one crucial way, though. The services that sit on top of it require a special digital token to operate. Using the internet analogy, it's as if each site on the web required visitors to acquire and spend a unique currency in order to access the site.

Another way to think of Ethereum is as an amusement park. Ethereum owns the park and lets others build and manage the rides. The apps for sports betting and file storage and so on are the rides. If you want to get on the betting roller coaster, you first have to buy and then cash in a roller coaster token. The file storage carousel likewise requires a file storage token. Ethereum helps the ride owners by minting their tokens. In return, the game owners pay Ethereum a small commission every time someone cashes in a token to get on a ride. Customers who come to the park can go on any ride they want, and go on multiple rides, but there is no all-access wristband: they must pay for each ride with that ride's special token, acquired at the Ethereum counter.

A quirk of this amusement park, however, is that most of the rides haven't been built yet, but customers still buy tokens for future rides. Using Ethereum, buyers acquired tokens in the hope that those tokens would *one day* be used for a blockchain service. In reality, the ride they buy into may or may not get built. But while they wait, they can always try and flip their tokens to someone else who wanted to bet on a ride getting built. And that's what most people did. Speculation pure and simple.

Every day in 2017, someone on the internet announced a new token project. And every day, people raced to buy the tokens. The projects spanned the lurid, including SpankChain, which promised a way to pay porn actors directly, to the far-fetched such as ASTRCoin, whose tokens purportedly served as claims on various asteroids. The phenomenon gained the name "the ICO." Instead of an IPO, or initial public offering, this was an "initial coin offering." The ICO could last a few days or a few weeks, and it involved sending funds—typically in Ethereum or bitcoin—to a project's online wallet and waiting to receive tokens in exchange.

Never in history has there been an easier way to raise more money from more people with such little effort. The number and size of the ICOs defied logic. Staggering sums changed hands every day. A company called Filecoin, which promised to build a blockchain storage network, raised $205 million. An outfit called Bancor, which touted an online supercurrency, raised $153 million worth of Ethereum in just three hours, while one called Brave—a new web browser—raised $35 million in thirty *seconds*. The flow of cash reached a crescendo with a service called EOS. Billing itself as a rival to Ethereum itself, EOS raised a staggering $4.2 *billion* with the marketing help of Brock Pierce, a former child star in Disney's Mighty Ducks movies, who had reinvented himself as a crypto gadfly.

Until 2017, the only companies that could raise that kind of capital were white-hot startups like Uber or Airbnb—"unicorns" in Silicon Valley slang. Sure, many claimed the likes of Uber were overvalued, but no one could deny what these startups did have: a proven business idea, millions of customers, and billions in revenue. Many of the ICO companies, by contrast, had none of these things. Millions were invested in small teams of developers with a white paper outlining their idea and nothing else. For their supporters, that was enough. After all, bitcoin and Ethereum had been born from nine-page white papers, and those projects were now worth billions. Why wouldn't these ICO projects produce the same result?

More than a few financial watchers who'd seen bubbles before pointed out that it was insane to throw hundreds of millions of dollars at these pop-up blockchain ventures. The *Financial Times'* influential Alphaville column spewed snark at ICOs and "crypto bros," warning it would all end in tears. But such doomsday prophecies from the financial establishment made little impression inside the bubble of Silicon Valley, where the tech elite were buzzing about an essay published by one of their own.

Titled "Thoughts on Tokens," the essay explained how ICO-style fundraising would help democratize finance and throw open the door to investments from around the globe: no longer would startups have to depend on a clique of venture capitalists to get off the ground. The high priests of Silicon Valley would soon be competing with a global base of token buyers to invest in new companies. The essay's author was Balaji Srinivasan—the same Balaji Srinivasan who had turned up at Coinbase three years before looking like a hobo/drug dealer with Ivy League ideas, and who was now a partner at the VC firm Andreessen Horowitz. "Thoughts on Tokens" zipped from inbox to inbox among the clubby world of Valley investors, triggering a rush of FOMO. Before long, the venture capital world began pouring money into an emerging crypto industry already awash in cash.

For the VCs, bets on crypto were a hedge of sorts. If Balaji was right, the forthcoming token economy was poised to upend the Valley's longtime role as kingmaker of the startup scene. Better then to try and get an inside track on the emerging industry that could make Sand Hill Road—the famous strip of Palo Alto and Menlo Park that houses the most prestigious venture capital offices—irrelevant.

Americans were glomming onto the growing crypto mania but it was nothing compared to what was happening across the Pacific. In South Korea, investing in crypto became as common as buying mutual funds, and by late 2017, one-third of the country's workers owned some sort of digital currency. A great number came from the country's lower-income strata—they called themselves "dirt spoons"—and saw owning crypto as a once-in-a-lifetime shot at subverting what they saw as a rigged class system. Korean television fanned the flames, producing spectacles like a game show where contestants competed to launch a new coin. In Japan, meanwhile, it was not just the young rushing to buy cryptocurrency. On the streets of Tokyo, retail stores sprang up to offer an easy way for seniors and others uneasy with technology to buy crypto. The stores removed the mystery of keys and wallets and blockchains, and instead allowed customers to walk up to a counter and purchase digital coins in the same way they would a bowl of noodles—a kind of brick-and-mortar version of Coinbase's user-friendly strategy.

By mid-2017, crypto stalwarts like bitcoin, Ethereum, and Litecoin were joined by a galaxy of new tokens that had flooded into the market through ICOs, with names like Qash or QuarkChain. No matter how obscure, nearly all promised they would be the next bitcoin—or at least something like it. In the case of Dentacoin, whose ICO raised $1.1 million, the project promised to be the crypto of choice for dentists. And in a market where crypto coins of all stripes kept soaring higher and higher, why not take a flyer on a brand-new ICO before the rest of the market bid up the price? Each day, it seemed, another obscure coin enjoyed a 100 percent pop, which in turn inspired yet another ICO.

The crypto media called this flood of new currencies "altcoins"—as in, alternatives to bitcoin. Longtime bitcoin believers had their own name for the tokens: "shitcoins." Shitcoin critics claimed the new tokens were spun up on shaky technology and then flogged in fly-by-night marketing schemes.

It was during this craze, at an exclusive investor conference in New York, that JPMorgan Chase CEO Jamie Dimon, likely horrified by the rampant speculation, tore into cryptocurrency, including bitcoin. He ranted that he would fire any employee trading bitcoin on the grounds of stupidity. Cryptocurrency wouldn't end well, he warned. "It's a fraud," he added for good measure. "Worse than tulip bulbs."

The market cared about neither Dimon's words nor the shitcoin critics. Prices kept climbing, and the ICOs kept multiplying. On Capitol Hill, Federal Reserve Chairman Janet Yellen testified before Congress—only to be photobombed by a prankster holding up a yellow legal pad with "Buy Bitcoin" scrawled across it. The image of Yellen looking stern as "Buy Bitcoin" floated like a thought bubble beside her head became another meme for the crypto community to flog. For his troubles, the prankster—known as bitcoin Sign Guy—earned six bitcoin in donations, or about $25,000.

By June, the price of bitcoin had tripled from the start of the year to reach an all-time high of $3,000, while Ethereum was up thirtyfold to $380. Many longtime crypto holders, who were now worth millions or tens of millions of dollars, cashed in portions of their hoard to invest in the new digital currencies on the market. Meanwhile, those who became staggeringly rich from an ICO often plowed their windfall into other ICOs, pumping still more money into the crypto craze.

A rising tide was lifting all boats, including Coinbase, which was signing up millions of new customers—whether it had the capacity to serve them or not.

* * *

In that June of 2016, life was good for Coinbase employees. The San Francisco weather was fine, and the ballooning value of their crypto and stock options felt finer still. Then on the morning of June 22, the bottom fell out. Employees stared at their screens in disbelief, then panic, then despair. A whale, bloated with the proceeds from a recent ICO, abruptly dumped millions of dollars' worth of Ethereum onto the company's GDAX exchange platform, causing the price to tumble. That caused others to sell, lowering the prices again and so on. Ethereum was in freefall. Its price on GDAX dropped from $320 to below $300 and then fell off a cliff, hurtling down to $13 and, for a brief moment, crashing to 10 cents.

It was a textbook example of a flash crash. A similar event had happened in 2010 on traditional exchanges when a London trader created fake trades to suggest an impending sell-off, triggering thirty minutes of chaos on US stock markets. The trader's antics fooled others in the market—most notably those who had put automatic "sell" orders in place in the event stocks fell below a certain price. These machine-triggered sell-offs led other machines to join the stampede to sell, regardless of the price and whether the sale was rational. Venerable companies like Procter & Gamble and Accenture briefly traded for mere pennies. The crash came to a halt when stock exchanges put a stop to all trading and then canceled transactions that had transpired during the machine-driven free-for-all.

The 2010 flash crash led major exchanges to adopt a system called *circuit breakers*, which automatically pause trading in the case of unusual, logic-defying fluctuations. Seven years later, no such system existed at Coinbase. Ironically, the company had carried out a tabletop simulation of a flash crash earlier that month, but no one had thought to install circuit breakers.

Adam White, who oversaw GDAX during the flash crash debacle, puts the blame on himself but also on amateurs in over their heads. These were so-called retail traders, who used GDAX's powerful platform to trade for their own accounts, as opposed to professional traders who traded on behalf of institutions for a living. "These retail guys can't protect themselves," White recalls. "It's like you give them a machine gun and find out they can't handle it."

It wasn't just retail investors who got burned with automated sell orders. So did many Coinbase employees who had set their GDAX accounts to sell Ethereum if it dipped below a certain price—and then watched in dismay as their automated sell order liquidated their position for a few dollars. Morale at the office plummeted in response to customer anger over the crash and to the financial wipeout that befell many on staff.

Two days later, Brian announced Coinbase would honor the trades that took place during the flash crash, while also reimbursing anyone who lost money from the haywire sell-offs—something of a lose-lose for Coinbase. This preserved goodwill among Coinbase customers on both sides of the ledger (and staff who thought they had lost it all). But the gesture cost Coinbase $20 million and later triggered an investigation from the CFTC.

The flash crash proved to be an expensive education for Coinbase, though the company was hardly alone in learning painful lessons during these months of crypto mania. Ordinary people were getting burned too, and unlike Coinbase's losses from the flash crash, their misfortune wasn't the result of honest mistakes. The boom had given birth to crypto predators who unleashed a series of brazen scams to part the greedy and the gullible from their money.

· · ·

"Bitcoooonnnnnect!" the voice boomed from the stage. "Hey, hey, hey! Whassup? Bitcoooooonnnnnect!"

The speaker, a trim, bald Latino man named Carlos Matos, beamed broadly. On the stage behind him, grinning hucksters clapped as Matos prowled back and forth, fronting a blue background and a large "Bitconnect" sign. Then he howled again.

"Bitcooooonnnnnect!" Matos bellowed to more cheers. Then the pitch: he recounted how he had used Bitconnect to turn $40,000 into $120,000 and would soon turn that into much, much more.

Matos had made his investment through a website that encouraged customers to trade in bitcoin and receive a new cryptocurrency— called Bitconnect—which they could lend out in order to receive returns as high as 40 percent a month. Customers could obtain even higher returns if they signed up other clients for Bitconnect. Crypto details aside, Bitconnect was an old-fashioned Ponzi scheme.

It worked for a while. Bitconnect tokens reached an all-time high in late 2017 of $450, but the value collapsed when the company shut down months later amid an FBI investigation. Today, its millions of tokens are worth nothing. The thousands of people who bought Bitconnect tokens, which briefly sat as the twentieth-most-popular cryptocurrency, lost every dollar. The only remaining value is Matos's "Bitcooooonnnnnect!" yodel, which became an internet meme and fodder for *Last Week Tonight*, John Oliver's late-night comedy takedown of current events.

Bitconnect investors weren't the only victims of crypto swindles. Others got fleeced by ICO exit scams, whose perpetrators did not even put up the pretext of running a company. Instead, they marketed the promise of a new cryptocurrency but stayed around only long enough to collect the ICO proceeds. After that, they vanished into the mists of the internet.

The scams were just so easy. All it took to spin up an ICO was a website and a white paper. In the most egregious examples, scammers would simply copy and paste technical jargon from other white papers and slap on a new title. Some websites dressed up the hustle with an ICO countdown clock, a marketing slogan, and biographies of the ICO team. The team profile was often fictitious, of course. More than a few ICO sites listed Ethereum founder Vitalik Buterin—who had nothing to do with the projects—as an executive or adviser.

Scammers with hacking skills found an even quicker way to profit from ICOs: hijack them. They'd quietly take control of an ICO's website and then, on the day when the fundraising commenced, change the payment address of the wallet designated to collect the bitcoin and Ethereum. The real ICO team could only watch in horror as the investors' funds got diverted into the hands of the hackers.

Coinbase, too, had to contend with hackers draining customer accounts. While the company had hardened its network against intruders, it could do little about customers who gave up control of their account passwords. Typically, this occurred as a result of phishing attacks on a client's Gmail account—similar to the one Russia directed at the Democratic political operative John Podesta prior to the 2016 election. Once a Coinbase customer's Gmail account was compromised, the hackers could ask to reset their password and steal their crypto.

Like banks and other sites, Coinbase required two-factor authentication—customers had to enter a code delivered to their phone before changing a password. Hackers found a way to get around this obstacle, however, by bribing employees at cell phone companies like AT&T. In exchange for a few dollars, a corrupt (or sometimes naive) employee would agree to change the SIM card associated with a customer's account. This would allow the hacker to intercept the authentication code that Coinbase sent out and burgle the customer's account. The scheme sounds elaborate, but it became so common in the crypto world it acquired a name—SIM-swapping—and would result in class action lawsuits against the phone carriers.

Other crooks targeted social media—a critical part of crypto culture—which became rife with criminal schemes. On Twitter, scammers created profiles with the faces of Brian and Vitalik, and announced they were giving away bitcoin and Ethereum in special promotions. To receive the windfall, the targeted Twitter user was told to send a small amount of cryptocurrency first—funds that would, of course, be promptly pocketed by the scammer. Twitter would eventually shut down the impersonator accounts, and the scammers would simply open new ones. The problem became so pervasive that Vitalik changed his Twitter name to "Vitalik Not Giving Away Ethereum Buterin."

On Telegram, the messaging app hugely popular with the crypto community, crooks organized conspiracies to manipulate the market. One Telegram group known as "the Big Pump" would pick a little-known altcoin and agree to buy it en masse. The influx of buyer interest, they hoped, would cause a stir in the market and lead naive outsiders to run in and buy the coin too, causing its value to soar. The Telegram insiders would then sell off their positions, completing the crypto version of a classic investment scam, the pump and dump. But those who joined the groups in hopes of a quick payout weren't actually in on the scheme. They were its victims. The organizers of groups like the Big Pump had already bought positions in the coin to be pumped, leaving the would-be conspirators to serve as patsies who would buy the coin at an inflated price. The crypto industry was so awash with dumb money that scammers were preying on scammers.

Crypto mania was out of control. The only thing that could have inflated it further was celebrity endorsements. And those came soon enough. On July 27, the boxer Floyd "Money" Mayweather posted an Instagram photo of himself on an airplane with a suitcase brimming with cash. "I'm gonna make a $hit t$on of money on August 2nd on the Stox.com ICO," he captioned it.

Few in the world of sports or even in crypto circles had heard of Stox, which purported to offer a blockchain-based way to make predictions on horse racing and other events. The company's obscure origins and half-baked business plan didn't deter the celebrity boxer who, in a follow-up Instagram post, told the world, "You can call me Floyd Crypto Mayweather from now on."

Soon after, the heiress Paris Hilton tweeted about her eager anticipation to participate in the launch of a token called Lydian that, in a perfect storm of buzzwords, promised to "deliver artificial intelligence marketing on a blockchain."

. . .

In Washington, DC, the Securities and Exchange Commission watched all the events of 2017 unfold with surprise and alarm. The blatant scams—and there were plenty of them—were bad, but so was the very premise of Initial Coin Offerings. After all, US law makes it illegal to sell securities to ordinary people without registering with the SEC—a process that's supposed to make companies follow rules related to accounting and transparency. Yet these ICOs appeared to be doing just that: selling securities. The promoters might call them coins and use a lot of blockchain lingo, but what they were selling looked for all the world like shares of stock or other securities.

Brian may have wanted to reimagine the SEC but what was happening with ICOs in some ways proved the value of what the SEC did on a day-to-day basis. Without its oversight, you get Bitconnect. You get pump-and-dumps. You get bribery, phishing, and SIM-swapping.

And the scale of it was staggering.

The trade publication *CoinDesk* reported that ICOs had pulled in $729 million in token sales in the second quarter of 2017 alone. That was more than triple the amount venture capitalists—the traditional financial engine of the startup word—had invested during the same period. And the ICO craze showed no sign of slowing.

In late July, the SEC broke its silence and issued a report concerning the DAO project—the autonomous investment service that had launched in 2016 and famously got hacked, triggering a rollback of the Ethereum blockchain. The hack had roiled the Ethereum world, but for the SEC, what mattered was that the DAO had begun as an ICO, issuing tokens to investors. And those tokens, said the SEC, amounted to a security sale.

The DAO report made clear that the SEC had at last arrived on the crypto scene. But it also amounted to no more than a warning shot. The SEC acknowledged that it had issued no rules about cryptocurrencies, so the organizers of the DAO had not technically broken the law. Thus, the agency would use the DAO episode to put other would-be token sellers on notice: The SEC would treat future ICOs as illegal unless the organizers first registered the coins with the agency.

This should have cooled the crypto fever sweeping the United States. It did not. A few months after the news came out, bitcoin hit another all-time high, near $5,000. Ethereum also soared, and so did the hundreds of altcoins riding in their wake. Brazen crypto promoters went forward with initial coin offerings all the same. The SEC is regarded as the powerful policeman of the financial markets. But during the crypto craze of 2017, the agency was caught off guard by the scale of the mania and came across as a mall cop pleading with a mob of rioting teens to settle down.

By the second half of 2017, crypto fever had burst into the mainstream. The business network CNBC started producing breathless reports on a daily basis about how to buy bitcoin. Fly-by-night PR agencies popped up, offering to promote new token sales via "ICO in a box" packages. And cunning lawyers conjured up a legal arrangement called a SAFT—short for Simple Agreement for Future Tokens—that they promised could circumvent the SEC's recent declaration that ICOs amounted to security sales.

Meanwhile, the sight of Lamborghinis became more common in crypto hubs like New York and San Francisco. The luxury car— already a brazen declaration of wealth—had become a talisman in the crypto community that revered the phrase "When Lambo? When Lambo?" as shorthand for "When are my tokens going through the roof?" Thanks to crypto prices that had shot up tenfold or more, the answer to "When Lambo?" became *"Now* Lambo" for dozens of young men who became stupid rich. Lamborghini posted more than a 10 percent year-over-year increase in sales.

A final dose of fuel for the crypto craze came with the launch of a spin-off from Bitcoin called Bitcoin Cash. The arrival of Bitcoin Cash came as unfinished business stemming from the long-running civil war over bitcoin block size that began back in 2015. A faction of Chinese miners, unhappy with bitcoin's ongoing congestion problem, had pushed through a plan to launch a new version of the currency with bigger blocks.

The launch of Bitcoin Cash meant engineering a hard fork—a radical software update like the one Ethereum had undergone a year before—that would lead to the creation of two rival blockchains. Though the fork was unpopular with the majority of longtime bitcoin believers, the big-block dissidents had enough influence to direct a critical mass of miners to work on their rival currency.

The upshot was that when Bitcoin Cash arrived on the scene, it sprang from nowhere to become the fourth-most-valuable cryptocurrency, worth billions. It also meant that anyone who held bitcoin prior to the split received an equal amount of the new currency as a pure windfall. It was like handing out a large cash dividend to stock owners in the midst of an improbable bull run. Many who received Bitcoin Cash sold it and plowed the proceeds right back into other parts of the overheated market.

Crypto prices, already tethered to little in the way of real-world value, kept climbing. And investors kept buying. The crypto spree of 2017 made the stock buying of the 1990s dot-com boom—famously described by then Federal Reserve Chair Alan Greenspan as "irrational exuberance"—look relatively sane.

It fell to Olaf, who was riding high at his crypto hedge fund since leaving Coinbase, to put an exclamation point on the era. He graced the cover of *Forbes* magazine, his shaggy blond mane set against a suit coat. In the photo, tossing coins casually, he fixes his elfish stare on the camera. Underneath, big block letters pronounce: "The Craziest Bubble Ever."

12

Coinbase Crackup

Nathalie's finger hovered over the "send" button. As Coinbase's longtime HR maven, she had written the email weeks earlier, and desperately hoped it would stay in her draft folder forever. But the bomb threat Coinbase had received that morning was more chilling and more credible than any of the previous ones. She stared at the ominous all-caps email telling the entire staff to flee the building but stay calm. Should she hit send? She had to decide.

As she sat at her desk in Coinbase's spacious open office high above San Francisco, Nathalie wondered just when the company had changed. Since joining the company as chief of staff at the ramshackle Bluxome Street apartment three years ago, she had risen to director and was on her way to becoming a vice president. The title was good, and the money was better. Yet she missed the early days when Coinbase felt less corporate and she could lead activities—hot-tub parties in Napa or fire-spinning classes in the city—with Brian and Olaf and a small crew who felt like family. Security mattered less back then, too. On

Bluxome Street, you had to deal with the odd kook knocking at the door. Now, Coinbase was hiring former FBI agents and drafting emails to deal with emergency evacuations.

Nathalie wasn't the only one on edge. Philip Martin, the security director, saw it as his job to be paranoid, and these days that wasn't hard. "We had these weird packages that kept arriving at our P.O. box," he recalls. Meanwhile, the bomb threats and other violent messages became near-weekly events. One recent incident had caused a squad of SFPD officers to swarm Market Street outside the Coinbase building. It turned out to be a false alarm but only added to the growing sense of unease within the company.

In response to this latest threat, Nathalie conferred again with the security team. She moved the email back to her drafts folder. A bomb threat was a real risk, but so was spreading panic through the workplace. She prayed she had made the right decision.

There were other things to worry about too. Mike Lempres, the company's political fixer and a longtime Justice Department veteran, worried what would happen if organized crime set its sights on Coinbase. Control Risks, a security consulting firm, had recorded an average of two crypto-related kidnappings every quarter, with criminals choosing targets based on public reports of their wealth. "These guys' ignorance is an issue," says Lempres. "They think if they kidnap Brian, he'll give them bitcoin. Silicon Valley is really ill-suited to deal with old-school thugs like the Russian or Italian mafias."

Martin also worried that the growing publicity surrounding bitcoin, and therefore Coinbase, would attract crooks plotting physical robbery. That's one reason why, by 2017, Brian and other top crypto executives rarely appeared in public without a retinue of bodyguards. They also became well versed in emergency tactics, such as using code words in the case of kidnapping or violence.

On top of these security concerns, the company faced threats from its own customers. The bull market of 2017 had put a strain on Coinbase's capacities, leading to technical meltdowns like the June flash crash and to a growing backlog of support tickets. Customers seethed in emails and especially on online forums like Reddit, accusing the company of conspiratorial plots to steal their crypto. That wasn't the case, of course. Coinbase was simply swamped and couldn't keep up with the massive increase in transaction volume and flood of new customers. Like a brave dog paddling against a too-powerful current, Coinbase employees worked nights and weekends to keep the site running and clear the backlog. But the chaos unleashed by crypto mania just kept growing. And then came December.

*   *   *

On New Year's Day 2017, investors had cheered bitcoin's long-awaited return to $1,000. Eleven months later, the currency smashed through the $10,000 mark. Some of Wall Street's finest thinkers offered elegant technical explanations for the incredible gain. Quants at Goldman Sachs employed something called the Elliott Wave Theory to suggest that the run-up represented an "impulse wave pattern" typical of mass market psychology. A financial technician named J. C. Parets said the upswing mirrored the Fibonacci sequence, a famous mathematical pattern that occurs in seashells, pine cones, and other elements of the natural world. Others called it a speculative mania. Or simply a bubble.

A week into December, bitcoin broke $16,000, fueled in part by massive trading on exchanges in Seoul and Tokyo. In the United States, taxi drivers and personal trainers joined hedge funds and day traders in bidding up the price still higher.

The frenzy also fueled an eye-popping run on Ethereum, which brushed $1,000 by December, and XRP, which had begun the year worth half a penny and now sold for $3. Altcoins, shitcoins, anything plausibly related to blockchain soared in value. As for Litecoin, Charlie Lee's creation had popped after it was listed on Coinbase that summer, and by mid-December it cracked $350—up from $4 at the start of the year. In a moment of exquisite timing, Lee sold off his entire hoard right near the all-time high, reaping $20 million from his invention.

As prices climbed and climbed, Brian published a blog post in early December titled "Please Invest Responsibly" that dryly warned customers of the volatility associated with cryptocurrency investing. The market paid no heed whatsoever. Prices kept climbing.

Brian's call for responsible crypto investing wasn't just ineffective—it was hypocritical. Coinbase, after all, offered a service that made irresponsible investing easy: buying crypto with credit cards. While it was rash to invest in a market that screamed "bubble," it was downright reckless to put the purchases on a Visa or Mastercard. Brian may have been worried about what he was witnessing, but he wasn't above collecting a 4 percent service charge to people paying for their investments on high-interest plastic. JPMorgan Chase, Bank of America, and others that issued the credit cards became alarmed and would within weeks ban their use for crypto purchases—a sure sign that many buying crypto on credit were in tight financial straits.

The December insanity spurred other unintended and absurd consequences. The long-running civil war over bitcoin's block size had never been resolved, meaning only one megabyte's worth of transactions could be stuffed into every block, and a new block could still only be added to the blockchain every ten minutes. Now, as the number of users on the bitcoin network swelled by millions every week, what had been a minor nuisance swelled into an epic backlog. Take any choke point that's already heavily congested—say New York City's Lincoln Tunnel or the 405 in Los Angeles—and then add fifty times the traffic. That's what happened to bitcoin's blockchain. Its network ground to a virtual halt. This meant the only way to ensure a transaction made it onto the blockchain within a reasonable amount of time was to pay the bitcoin miners who maintained the ledger. With a captive, desperate customer base, those miners began demanding colossal premiums. Run-of-the-mill transactions became staggeringly expensive. On December 8, for example, a man named Kristian Freeman tweeted in dismay that sending $25 in bitcoin to a friend had triggered a $16 fee. Forty percent of his $41 transaction went to a service charge. Sure, a bitcoin user could refuse and offer a lowball fee. But this would mean waiting days for a transaction to clear—if it cleared at all.

• • •

Paradoxically, this moment of bitcoin's biggest success, when it burst into the mainstream like never before, also showcased its biggest failure. Satoshi's vision had promised a new and democratic form of internet-based money that could be used with few fees or constraints. The reality of bitcoin in December 2017, however, was a bloated and dysfunctional network that made Western Union wire transfers look cheap and efficient. Underscoring how impractical bitcoin had become, a major crypto conference in Miami that December declared it would not accept bitcoin as payment for entry.

By the time bitcoin crossed $15,000 in early December, the network was hopelessly clogged and transfer fees were astronomical. These facts did nothing to quell demand. The price continued to rise as much as $1,000 a day as frantic speculators bought more and more bitcoin. Everyone wanted to cash in, including companies that had nothing to do with crypto. An obscure beverage company called Long Island Iced Tea Corp. changed its name to the Long Blockchain Corp. The pivot boosted its share price 200 percent—and later, it brought an insider trading investigation from the SEC and a delisting from NASDAQ.

On December 17, the currency brushed against the unfathomable high point of $20,000. A single bitcoin was now worth the same as a pound of gold. On CNBC, the network had given over half of its airtime to the mania, sweeping aside staid coverage of stocks and bonds in favor of bringing on crypto pundits who of course predicted bitcoin would soar even higher.

· · ·

Half the world, it seemed, was getting into crypto. And for many of those people, their first stop was Coinbase. In February 2014, the company counted one million customers and now, just under four years later, it had twenty million. On most days that December, more than one hundred thousand people signed up for their first Coinbase wallet.

Inside the company's Market Street headquarters, Adam White recalls employees high-fiving as Coinbase notched a day with $4 billion worth of transactions. They whooped over reported daily revenue numbers. Meanwhile, Coinbase became the most downloaded app in iPhone's App Store, a moment that was particularly sweet given how, not so long ago, Apple had turfed the company out of its App Store for offering crypto trading. Now Coinbase was more popular than Facebook or Twitter.

Coinbase was making waves with venture capitalists. It was also making money—lots of it. The company was processing millions of transactions of bitcoin, Ethereum, and Litecoin, and it took a cut of each one. The company's margins were huge. While Coinbase had to spend a lot on engineers, the actual cost of performing a transaction—moving digital dust in and out of customers' wallets—was almost zero. When a customer bought $100 of bitcoin, Coinbase could charge $2.99, and that was effectively pure profit.

"The first time I met him, Brian said, 'I want to build a billion-dollar business,'" recalls Katie Haun, the former prosecutor turned Stanford crypto professor, who had recently joined the Coinbase board. Now, Brian had achieved that goal. The December surge in sign-ups meant Coinbase would book more than $1 billion in revenue in 2017 while, months earlier, it had taken its place as a unicorn—a startup valued at more than a billion dollars. And Coinbase wasn't just any unicorn—a leak from board member Barry Schuler months later revealed it was worth $8 billion, making it one of the ten most valuable startups in the country. What Uber was to ride-hailing and what Airbnb was to home rentals, Coinbase was to crypto.

For Brian, all of this was vindication for the open secret he'd seized on at Y Combinator six years before. He had recognized that many more people would buy bitcoin if given an easy way to do it, and the success of Coinbase had proved him right. And now he had also realized a long-burning ambition—an ambition that had inflamed the tech visionaries who put their stamp on his hometown of San Jose and the famous valley that stretches north of it.

As the price of bitcoin reached its all-time high, Brian's company had become a money-printing machine. The machine, however, had been overheating for a while. And amid the massive influx of customers during December, the money machine threatened to explode and take out Coinbase with it.

• • •

"We were all good software engineers, but none of us knew infrastructure," says Coinbase's second employee, Craig Hammell, explaining how the company had been built the Silicon Valley way—quickly and with whatever tools could help it add customers in a hurry. These included tools startups know well, like MongoDB to manage data and Heroku for apps. Such tools are fine for scaling a startup but not for processing millions of sensitive transactions. Coinbase was using West Coast coding to do the crypto equivalent of East Coast banking. Scaling up a dating app is one thing. Managing millions of people's money is another. "This type of engineering was tough stuff. Things like MongoDB were OK for prototyping but not for a major financial operation," says Charlie Lee.

In building Coinbase, it was as if Brian and the other engineers had constructed a finely designed California beach house and then plunked it down on the coast of Maine during a nor'easter. That house wouldn't survive a battering from the howling wind and snow. The owners would rue the fact they hadn't used better building materials as the house shook and creaked and, eventually, cracked. This was the state of Coinbase's website in December 2017. Juan Suarez, the company's longtime lawyer, recalls flying to Pittsburgh for a family Christmas visit only to land and receive an urgent message from Brian to turn around immediately: "The feeling was like, 'Oh shit.' It's like we were on this bluff overlooking the ocean all by ourselves and all the crosswinds in the world were bearing down on us."

Prior to December, customer trades had been getting delayed as parts of the website began to buckle. The influx of millions of new users in the days before Christmas, however, crashed the site, and it stayed down for hours at a time. Client orders ended up in technical purgatory. Angry users fumed on Reddit and Twitter.

Banking partners who took their deposits contributed to some of Coinbase's technical snafus. Its biggest European partner, an Estonian bank called LHV, did not use APIs (application programming interfaces)—a standard way for computers to communicate with each other—but instead required Coinbase to manually upload transactions in a spreadsheet. Coinbase engineers wrote scripts to automatically fill the spreadsheets, only to discover they could upload just fifty items at a time. It was like trying to do calculus on an abacus.

Wherever the fault lay, disgruntled customers and ideological foes took out their frustrations on Coinbase, directing waves of malicious traffic at its website to knock it offline.

Underscoring the technical misery was a leadership vacuum. Even as the company's business volume more than quadrupled, its executive ranks thinned. Fred's leaving in January deprived Coinbase of the military-style efficiency he had helped create in its early days, while Olaf's departure meant the loss of its chief internal diplomat. Olaf had the unusual quality—especially in ego-driven Silicon Valley—of being liked by absolutely everyone with whom he worked, a quality that made him invaluable in spotting problems and smoothing over office conflicts. By November, as trading volumes began to surge, Brian had only two longtime executives—Adam White and the general manager of Coinbase's consumer division, Dan Romero—to help him avert a total meltdown. The lack of an executive suite, and the company's mounting customer service problems, did not go unnoticed by Coinbase's board, who began receiving emails from friends complaining about the disorder at the company.

Chris Dixon and other members of the board came up with what they hoped was a solution. Just as the eccentric Google founders had once needed what Silicon Valley calls "adult supervision"—and received it in the form of a veteran CEO, Eric Schmidt—the Coinbase board sent help in the form of Asiff Hirji, a veteran banking and telecom executive who had since taken a post at VC titan Andreessen Horowitz.

Hirji arrived in November during the speculative mania and just before the December insanity as Coinbase's first chief operating officer.

It was like starting a new job in the midst of a five-alarm fire. "They couldn't cope with the scale," he says. "The company had grown 40 times over that year. We didn't know how much cash we had on hand, plus or minus $200 million, which is ridiculous."

Hirji was also aghast at Coinbase's financial infrastructure. He had seen his share of firms blow up as a result of relying on unconventional trading software and, when he first looked under the hood of Coinbase, he feared it would suffer the same fate. But in the trading frenzy of December, any major fixes would have to wait—it would be like trying to swap out a fighter jet's engine midair. All Coinbase could do was hold on and hope.

• • •

A growing number of customers, however, were out of patience. More and more orders were getting delayed or vanishing—a maddening experience when the price of bitcoin was swinging by thousands of dollars in a day. Customers were stuck wondering if their order had been fulfilled at the rate of $16,000 or $19,000 per bitcoin, or if it had been fulfilled at all. Anger bred conspiracy theories; some believed Coinbase's technical problems were just a ruse to steal their money— and they vowed revenge for this imagined crime. "We had these people saying, 'We're going to come to your office and blow it up and shoot everyone,'" Nathalie recalls.

Linda Xie, a longtime Coinbase product manager, shudders when she recalls anti-Coinbase zealots on Reddit posting sinister photos of employees and the company's office. Their fury would boil over not only online but also on the streets of San Francisco. Soon, she stopped disclosing her identity at crypto meetups in the city, fed up with being accosted by random strangers angry at Coinbase. It took a toll.

"I was surprised how much it affected the leadership team," says Linda. It made me realize how human people were—they were reading all the Reddit comments and taking it to heart, being saddened by what they read. People thought Coinbase was a black hole and that no one was listening."

Coinbase's ham-handed approach to customer service didn't help. Even in the early days, the company had not been adept at addressing complaints—its first approach had involved Olaf fending off thousands of emails by writing an automated program in which a fictitious person, Roger, would respond to them. Years later, when Brian finally recognized the company needed a director of customer support, he didn't turn to a newly minted MBA or a retail veteran. He turned to Reddit, using an online quiz to recruit candidates to fill the position.

The new director was, in Nathalie's words, "a lovely human who likes to be introverted." Hardly ideal for customer service. Additional members of the customer support team were added primarily because they loved bitcoin—a suitable quality for an online crypto company, of course, but not a quality necessarily helpful in calming legions of furious customers.

Typically, when situations reach crisis levels like this, Valley startups turn to PR firms that specialize in both the tech world and crisis communications to help fix, or at least contain, the problem. Brian, however, found media relations to be a waste of time and energy, preferring to focus on engineering matters. But as media demands became more insistent during 2017, he deputized a Coinbase engineer, David Farmer, to deal with it. Farmer, who knew nothing about communications, loathed the task and could only grit his teeth in annoyance as an avalanche of reporters' emails demanded to know why the company appeared to be melting down.

On December 19, Bitcoin Cash—the bitcoin spin-off with the bigger blocks—became available for Coinbase customers to buy and sell.

The new offering went haywire almost instantly as prices unexpectedly soared, in part because of a flood of "buy" orders. It turns out that many customers had ordered buys to be made no matter what the price was when it became available. Only four hours after launching Bitcoin Cash, Coinbase had to halt trading to sort out the mess—creating even more angry customers. Others had noticed an unusual price spike in Bitcoin Cash that had occurred hours before Coinbase announced trading for the currency. It was easy for conspiracy-minded fanatics to connect the dots. At the least, the activity looked suspicious and fanned further rage on social media. A typical tweet:

> I don't care how you slice it, this is INSIDER TRADING! Someone with a lot of bitcoin knew @coinbase would add bitcoin Cash BCH and took one BIG chunk of profit from [it]. Whoever you are you are your making crypto look like Wall Street. Shame on you.

In response to the uproar, Brian declared Coinbase had a zero-tolerance policy for trading on inside information and announced an internal investigation. The company would find no evidence of wrongdoing. But behind the scenes, Coinbase executives quietly vaporized a channel on Slack—the company's internal messaging system—called "Trading Strategies," in which employees swapped ideas about how to make money from crypto trading.

In 2018, angry shareholders filed a class action lawsuit over the Bitcoin Cash debacle. The following year, a federal judge would declare Coinbase should stand trial for negligence.

. . .

By December 31, just two weeks after bitcoin touched the sun at $20,000, all cryptocurrencies were in a flat spin. Bitcoin had plunged

35 percent from its all-time high, and most expected it to continue its corrective plummet. A drop in trading volume had eased the problem of exorbitant transfer fees, though transactions remained slow and expensive. And Coinbase was still drowning in a morass of technical problems and customer rage.

As a short, gloomy day in San Francisco drew to a close, Brian made a new attempt to address the crises that had battered Coinbase. He went to the place he knew and where he felt at home: Reddit. His post began: "Coinbase CEO here—our support is very backed up. . . . Someone will respond to your support request, although it may take some time. Your coins are not 'lost.' Apologies for the delay, it is definitely not the experience we want to be providing to our customers."

PART THREE

From Crypto Winter to the Crypto Future

13

Hangover

"The telephone blasted Peter Fallow awake inside an egg with the shell peeled away and only the membranous sac holding it intact. Ah! The membranous sac was his head, and the right side of his head was on the pillow, and the yolk was as heavy as mercury, and it rolled like mercury, and it was pressing down on his right temple and his right eye and his right ear. If he tried to get up to answer the telephone, the yolk, the mercury, the poisoned mass, would shift and roll and rupture the sac, and his brains would fall out."

—**Tom Wolfe,** *The Bonfire of the Vanities*

Wolfe's account has been cited as the greatest hangover in fiction. It's also a good analogy for the cryptocurrency industry at the start of 2018. The market was in free fall as bitcoin lost half its value, sinking below $10,000 by February, and the state of altcoins was even worse. But for a few months, big investors could pretend the bubble had not popped—they could pray, like Wolfe's hangover subject, that there was no rupture and that all the money would not leak away.

It was harder for small-time investors to nurture such illusions. Most were people who came to crypto late in the game—buying bitcoin on a credit card for $15,000 or $18,000 or plowing savings into a shitcoin ICO. They could only watch in despair as prices kept plunging. By April, bitcoin fell below $7,000 and kept falling. Many other digital currencies, backed only by a white paper and lofty promises, were down 90 percent or more and would never recover. Buyers of exotic tokens like Emercoin or XEM suffered the same fate as those who bought Dutch tulip futures in the seventeenth century or stock in the South Sea Company in the eighteenth. Like these unlucky Europeans of yore, the crypto buyers were victims of a modern-day speculative bubble, without even the flowers to show for it. They had traded cash for digital dust.

In 2017, the media offered numerous accounts of ordinary individuals who had ridden the crypto wave to windfalls. Now, the stories took a sadder turn. The *New York Times* told of the hard lessons learned by an Englishman who had thrown his savings of $23,000 into altcoins and now held only $4,000. On Reddit, the stories were darker. One user told a discussion board how his wife had left him after he dumped all of their money into Tron, a once-hyped altcoin that hit a high of 23 cents but now trades for a penny. Other Reddit readers consoled each other with assurances that the market would bounce back or, in some cases, shared the numbers of suicide prevention hotlines. In Asia, which had been ground zero for crypto mania, the misery was particularly widespread. In one widely shared news story, a Korean mother in the city of Busan recounted how her twenty-year-old son took his life after months of trading cryptocurrencies.

Even as amateur and small-time crypto buyers reeled, others greeted 2018 as if the 2017 party remained in full swing. The mercurial investor Peter Thiel revealed his Founder's Fund had taken a $20 million position in bitcoin. Venture capitalists disclosed deals they had hatched at the height of the mania, including a $75 million investment by billionaire Tim Draper's fund into Ledger, a company that makes crypto storage devices. ICOs had not gone completely out of style—the messaging app Telegram declared it would raise $500 million by selling its own tokens. And in a Hail Mary gambit, the CEO of Kodak—the once-proud camera maker from upstate New York—announced it would back KodakCoin, a half-baked scheme to manage photographs on the blockchain.

The cultural excesses of crypto mania would linger well after the bubble had popped. At Consensus, the crypto industry's annual trade show, Lamborghini owners parked conspicuously on Manhattan's Sixth Avenue to kick off the event. Inside, fly-by-night companies crowded airless hallways in the hopes of finding the dumb money that had sloshed around so freely just months before. Meanwhile, sixteen hundred miles away, a gaggle of wealthy twenty-something men had descended upon Puerto Rico. Their arrival came as residents of the island struggled to rebuild from the devastation wreaked by Hurricane Maria, but the young millionaires—some of them were billionaires— had another priority: creating "Puertopia." This was to be a new type of city where people paid only with cryptocurrency and laws were written on a blockchain. For the new arrivals, Puertopia invoked a paradise. For everyone else, it meant "crypto bros looking for a tax haven." The plan would unravel less than two years later when the island's corrupt governor, a supporter of the scheme, resigned in disgrace.

Even as its economic foundation crumbled in early 2018, crypto continued to garner attention in the media and popular culture. This included a profile of Vitalik Buterin in "Lunch with the FT"—the *Financial Times* column where typical subjects included the likes of Jeff Bezos, Angela Merkel, and Angelina Jolie. In the profile, the Ethereum founder recounts a recent tête-à-tête he had with Russian President

Vladimir Putin about crypto and laments the greed that engulfed many ICOs. "There's projects that never had a soul, that are just like, 'ra-ra, price go up. Lambo, vrromm, buybuybuy now'!" exclaimed Buterin, whose eccentricity had only grown with his Ethereum fame.

By the spring of 2018, Hollywood scriptwriters had glommed onto the fading days of crypto mania as well. In the show *Billions*, the main character Bobby Axelrod, who is reportedly based on real-life hedge fund billionaire Steve Cohen, turns to cryptocurrency to thwart SEC trading restrictions. "One million dollars straight in crypto, in chilly storage," Bobby says, proffering a USB storage device to a minion.

A few days later, HBO's tech parody, *Silicon Valley*, would likewise air an episode that uses cryptocurrency as a central plot point. The episode depicts a main character, Bertram Gilfoyle, plunging forward with a plan to mine and distribute "Pied Piper Coins"—tokens named for his company—through an ICO. Pied Piper Coin would earn a place in crypto lore, but it would not be the most famous fictional coin to launch in 2018. Days after the Pied Piper episode, the crypto world buzzed with news of another ICO called "HoweyCoin." The coin's website purported to offer a new type of crypto that could be used for travel or bought and sold as an investment. And in true ICO fashion, the HoweyCoin website included an offer for investors to receive discounted coins if they purchased early.

HoweyCoin, however, turned out to be a clever prank played by the Securities and Exchange Commission to call attention to the perils of ICOs. The name "Howey" was a tongue-in-cheek reference to a Supreme Court case about the sale of securities, and anyone gullible enough to try and purchase HoweyCoins would be redirected to an SEC page that warned about sketchy investments.

It's not every day that a federal regulator trolls an entire industry, so the HoweyCoin episode earned the SEC plenty of publicity. The fake

Howey site even included an endorsement from a famous boxer—a not-so-subtle riff on Floyd "Crypto" Mayweather's vow the previous year to "make a shit-ton of money" on an ICO.

The SEC, it turned out, had a sense of humor, but that didn't mean there was anything funny about the wave of enforcement the agency was unleashing on the crypto industry. Like a slumbering grizzly bear poked again and again, the SEC was at last awake and ready to mete out punishments.

In January, SEC Chairman Jay Clayton sent chills down the spines of many in the crypto industry with a speech to an annual gathering of securities lawyers. The chairman called the behavior of certain attorneys involved in ICOs "disturbing," and scolded them for enabling the hucksters. "There are ICOs where the lawyers involved appear to be, on the one hand, assisting promoters in structuring offerings of products that have many of the key features of a securities offering, but call it an 'ICO,' which sounds pretty close to an 'IPO.' On the other hand, those lawyers claim the products are not securities, and the promoters proceed without compliance with the securities laws," scolded Clayton.

Translation: *You guys are supposed to advise your clients not to sell this crap—not help them unload it.*

The SEC had tried to telegraph this message in July 2017 with its warning that the ICO project known as the DAO had dealt in unlicensed securities. But few in the crypto world knew or cared about the SEC's salvo. Not long after the July warning, a clever lawyer named Marco Santori had unveiled a document called the SAFT (short for Simple Agreement for Future Tokens). The SAFT was a riff on a familiar startup investment contract known as SAFE (Simple Agreement for Future Equity)—and this SAFT version promised a safe and legal path to holding an ICO. Thanks to the SAFT, it looked like the ICO party could go on.

Santori's aggressive approach to crypto lawyering had already earned him a plum position at Cooley, a prominent Silicon Valley law firm that has long come up with creative ways to accommodate the tech industry. In the dot-com boom, for instance, Cooley became one of the first firms to accept equity from startups instead of cash retainers. It's no surprise, then, that Santori and his magical SAFT agreement appeared to be a perfect fit for the firm—until the SEC Chairman's fateful speech about lawyers abetting the sale of unlicensed securities. Shortly after the speech, Santori's short stint at Cooley came to an abrupt end.

The reputation of ICOs, meanwhile, dimmed further. At the *Wall Street Journal*, investigative reporters had pored over the documents for more than fourteen hundred ICOs and uncovered some grim findings: 271 of them had red flags, such as plagiarized filings or fake executive profiles that showed pictures cribbed from stock photo sites. Plenty of people had warned that the ICO economy was rife with scams, but now there was a growing pile of evidence.

The *Wall Street Journal* report appeared as San Franciscans and New Yorkers alike basked in the glorious days of late spring. But in crypto circles, they were calling this period of time "crypto winter." The phrase sprang from the lips of depressed investors and ricocheted around social media. As crypto prices continued to slide ever downward, it became clear the chill of crypto winter would not yield to a spring for a long time to come.

· · ·

A burst of investment in crypto in early 2018, such as Peter Thiel's $20 million bet, convinced some that the bubble hadn't burst, but by May it became clear that the good times were over. Retail investors who had made smaller bets on crypto felt the pain first; the big players came next. Masayoshi Son, the founder of Japanese conglomerate SoftBank, had also bought at the top of the bitcoin market only to take a drubbing to the tune of $130 million when he sold off his position months later. Goldman Sachs, the investment bank whose aversion to tech had led Fred Ehrsam to quit in frustration, had finally, it appeared, come around to bitcoin. After a series of press leaks teasing the news, Goldman revealed that it was creating a desk to trade cryptocurrency and, as if to underscore the edginess of the gambit, appointed a smirking thirty-eight-year-old with a man-bun to head the desk. The gambit, however, was short-lived. The bank quietly pulled the plug months later.

Crypto's moment in the mainstream had passed. Whatever toes had been dipped in the pool were withdrawn. Once again, the biggest names of the financial establishment wanted no part of it. As if to underscore the point, Warren Buffett explained to investors in May that bitcoin was "probably rat poison squared," while his longtime consigliere, Charlie Munger, likened cryptocurrency trading to "dementia." (Buffett's opinion was no doubt reinforced two years later when a cryptocurrency CEO won an auction to attend the Oracle of Omaha's annual charity lunch, but then canceled amid reports he was being investigated by the Chinese government.)

The fallout from crypto winter spread to unlikely places. On the sweeping plains of Rockdale, Texas, town leaders had extended their finest southern hospitality to woo the crypto-mining giant Bitmain to set up shop. The arrival of Bitmain brought the promise of hundreds of well-paying jobs to a place that had been hard hit by the closing of an Alcoa coal plant. To clinch the deal, Rockdale's political leaders ginned up a ten-year tax abatement plan for the firm and feted Bitmain executives at banquets with beer and Texas barbecue.

"We'll feed and water you," drawled the county judge to their would-be crypto saviors. But the Texans' high hopes came crashing down as crypto prices kept falling, and Bitmain concluded its mining venture would not pan out.

As 2018 dragged to a close, the smart-money set began to get wiped out too. Hedge funds, which months earlier had splashed onto the financial scene, began to close their doors. By year's end, more than three dozen crypto funds would shut for good, while one of the most prominent funds—billionaire Mike Novogratz's Galaxy Digital—would post an eye-popping loss of $272 million for the year. Even Olaf, who enjoyed prophet status in many corners of the crypto world, couldn't escape the mounting malaise. An unflattering profile appeared in the *Wall Street Journal*, portraying Olaf as a dilettante weirdo and his Polychain Capital fund as floundering in losses and legal trouble. The profile showed Olaf looking defiant in front of a bookshelf that displayed two copies of *Infinite Jest*.

• • •

On Market Street, Brian and Coinbase also endured crypto winter. A total collapse in prices—bitcoin would tumble a full 85 percent to just over $3,000 by December of 2018—delivered a gut-punch to the company's income. Despite its long-running quest to find new revenue streams, Coinbase still lived very much on trading commissions, and a 3 percent cut on $3,000 obviously didn't compare to the 3 percent it took on $20,000. And they were taking fewer commissions: client activity had fallen 80 percent since the go-go days of the previous December.

Coinbase's problems beyond the slump were mounting, too. The company's run-and-gun, just-hold-on approach during the bubble had produced a fine legal mess. Bitcoin Cash customers were suing over the December debacle. The IRS was still rooting around in Coinbase's client files. And to top it off, angry customers had filed over one hundred complaints with the SEC accusing the company of mishandling their money. Coinbase was in constant contact with its white-shoe law firm Davis Polk, where partners bill $2,000 an hour. The cost of pissing off clients and the government was becoming very, very expensive.

Despite all this, Coinbase had reason to be optimistic. The company's finances were in good shape thanks to a series E funding round worth $300 million and backed by the hedge fund Tiger Global. This cash infusion topped off a war chest the company had built up during the boom. Unlike other high-profile startups like Uber and WeWork, which were bleeding billions every quarter, Coinbase could actually turn a profit. Meanwhile, Coinbase lacked the hyper-bro culture that contributed to the implosion of other startups, including WeWork, whose plans for an IPO blew up spectacularly amid reports of its CEO's penchant for tequila shots and smoking weed.

What's more, crypto winter offered Coinbase a desperately needed respite. If 2017 had been a wildly successful party, then 2018 would be a year to clean up all the broken glass and replace the smashed furniture. For Coinbase, the calm offered time to patch up buggy code and fix its long-running customer service problem. "Things operate differently during peacetime than wartime," says Brian. He remained optimistic. For others, the crash was apocalyptic. For him, 2018 looked like the slump of 2015, when many had written off the crypto industry for dead. He would move forward and use the new downturn as an opportunity to retool for an upswing.

This retooling involved ceding some control to Asiff Hirji, the COO who had arrived in November as part of the push by Coinbase's board to introduce adult supervision to the company. It didn't take him long to get to work. In Asiff's view, Coinbase had come within a whisker of complete collapse in December of 2017 as a result of three critical risks: inadequate insurance coverage; a chaotic accounting system that made it impossible to tell if the company was up or down $200 million; and a jerry-rigged proprietary trading system known as "the hedger" that could blow up any minute.

The first two risks could be addressed easily enough. As part of the adult supervision mandate, Asiff brought on a chief financial officer, Alesia Haas, who smoothed out the insurance and accounting snafus. The hedger was another matter.

It was Fred Ehrsam who had introduced the hedger in the first place, back in the days when Coinbase lacked its own exchange and had to source bitcoins on the open market. The system used the company's homespun algorithms to determine optimal times to buy and sell crypto. This not only provided the cash liquidity Coinbase needed to run its everyday operations, but also for arbitrage opportunities—chances to profit from small differences in price between different banks and exchanges.

The homegrown hedger was a source of pride for longtime Coinbase hands. To Asiff, it was a source of fear and dread. "In December," he recalls, "the hedger misbehaved and almost melted down the company. I've seen it before—it's a guaranteed way for trading companies to blow up, using those proprietary systems. There's some misconfiguration of the algorithm, and no one knows what's getting bought and sold. I went on a crusade to kill the hedger."

Asiff won his crusade. Soon the hedger was dead and Coinbase was using an agency trading model—accepting a trade only when the other half of the trade was there in the market. In Asiff's view, he had saved the company by extricating it from a trading model that relied on a black box that could blow up at any moment.

More and more, Coinbase's leadership looked like a typical corporation. The executive team at Coinbase, which for years had amounted to Brian and Fred and a loose mantra of running through brick walls, added veteran outsiders. Asiff poached Emilie Choi, a longtime veteran of LinkedIn, and anointed her as VP of business development with the mission of acquiring a host of smaller crypto companies. He appointed a VP of communications, Rachael Horowitz, a firebrand who was fazed by nothing after navigating years of crises at Facebook and Twitter. (With Horowitz on board, David Farmer, the economist deputized to handle media by Brian, and who hated public relations, would no longer have to endure reporters' calls.) As if to underscore its new posture to the press, the company also added Elliott Suthers, a caustic Australian who had earned his PR chevrons coaching onetime Republican candidate Sarah Palin for vice presidential debates.

Brian was freed from managing every last thing. Finally, he had time to pursue personal activities. He took flying lessons and dated actresses. And still committed to his longtime passion for using bitcoin to spread financial autonomy through the world, he launched a philanthropic fund, Give Crypto. Analytical as ever, Brian subscribed to research that suggested the best way to alleviate poverty was to give money to people who are poor. Give Crypto, he declared, would raise $1 billion for the cause.

As Asiff built the corporate team and Brian nurtured noble ambitions to save the world, the hangover persisted. Crypto winter dragged on. Safe in its financial fortress, Coinbase waited patiently for spring. Nearly too late, the company would realize this was a terrible mistake.

14

"Getting Our Asses Kicked"

T oo much success makes you not as hungry. Not as disciplined. Not as paranoid," Olaf says, sipping tea in a Manhattan restaurant in 2019.

It's been years since the day he first turned up for work at Coinbase with a single Uniqlo dress shirt to his name. Olaf doesn't look boyish anymore, but his eyes still sparkle with the same intensity, and he's as eager as ever to talk about lucid dreaming. Now in his early thirties, Olaf has the improbable task of managing money for Andreessen Horowitz and other high-wattage VC firms through his crypto fund, Polychain Capital. He still cares deeply about Coinbase—he and Brian are close friends—but frets about what his former employer has grown into.

"Coinbase got too comfortable," he adds. "At a board meeting, it was all about, 'How are we going to spend all this money in order to avoid a tax liability?'" In Olaf's view, Coinbase should have been exploring the new frontiers of crypto rather than perfecting its corporate finance game.

• • •

The cash bonanza of 2017, it turned out, did create complacency. Coinbase entered the crypto winter believing it could simply wait for the next upswing while spending its time snapping up smaller companies and patching up its battered infrastructure. This was a sensible tactic but a poor strategy. As Coinbase sat back and waited for the market to turn, it failed to account for rapid changes that were happening in crypto even during the downturn—changes that threatened to make Coinbase obsolete. The company was like a driver tuning up an old Buick even as, in a garage next door, his rival was detailing a Porsche.

Brian's new rival went by the name of CZ (the initials stand for Changpeng Zhao, but everyone uses the shorthand version). CZ wears wireless glasses and close-cropped black hair. In public, his go-to attire is a black hoodie emblazoned with the name of his company in yellow letters: BINANCE. Since he appeared on the scene in 2017, CZ has emerged as the most disruptive figure in the history of crypto after Satoshi and Vitalik.

CZ was born in the Chinese province of Jiangsu. He and his family crossed the Pacific when he was twelve years old to start a new life in Vancouver. The move was necessary after his father, a professor, run afoul of Chinese authorities for being too outspoken—a characteristic that, years later, would redound in his son's demeanor. In Canada, a teenage CZ dunked fries at McDonald's and worked overnight shifts at a gas station to help his family. All the while, he honed his natural aptitude for finance and computers.

CZ's coding prowess won him a ticket to McGill University's computer science program, and then gigs at major financial hubs around the globe. Like other prominent crypto figures, CZ embarked on a peripatetic existence—building software for the Tokyo Stock Exchange and then working for Bloomberg in New York before moving on to Beijing, where he built high-frequency trading tools.

It wasn't until 2013 that CZ, then thirty-six, discovered bitcoin. He became fascinated. His new passion led him to London and a stint with Blockchain, the crypto wallet company founded by Ben Reeves—the would-be cofounder of Coinbase whom Brian had jilted on the eve of startup school. In a karmic payback of sorts, Reeves would help launch the crypto career of the man who would become Brian's biggest rival.

CZ thrived at Blockchain and then at another crypto shop, OKCoin, but what he really wanted was to put his own stamp on the industry. He bided his time until, in 2017, he chose to strike. As ICO mania hit a peak, CZ launched a token offering of his own, raising $15 million to fund his new company, an exchange he called Binance.

Binance wasn't just any cryptocurrency exchange. In an ingenious twist on the business model, CZ encouraged customers to use Binance tokens—the ones he sold in the ICO—to obtain a discount on trading commissions. This meant the fee for a trade on Binance's exchange might cost $10 if a customer paid with bitcoin but only $5 if the fee was paid in Binance Coin. Unlike so many other new cryptocurrencies, CZ's coin was useful.

Owning Binance Coin was a bit like holding shares in ICE, the parent company of the New York Stock Exchange. The shares were an investment that would rise and fall based on how well the exchange was doing. But in the case of Binance Coin, the shares could also be used to purchases stocks listed on the exchange.

To further juice the value of his new currency, CZ had arranged for the exchange to destroy a given supply of Binance Coin every quarter. This served to reduce the overall supply of Binance Coin and drive up their price—the equivalent of corporate share buybacks in traditional finance.

In one stroke, CZ had devised a system to keep customers loyal to his exchange—the discounts on fees offered by Binance Coin—while also creating a valuable new currency. In the months after the ICO, the coin's market cap would cross $1 billion and, by 2019, would become the sixth-most valuable cryptocurrency. CZ himself joined Brian and the Winklevoss twins as a crypto billionaire.

A big reason for this success was another clever move by CZ: he decided Binance would eschew the business of trading conventional currency—dollars, euros, yen—for crypto and offer only crypto-to-crypto trades. This meant customers could swap bitcoin for Ethereum, or Ethereum for Litecoin, or Litecoin for dozens of other cryptocurrencies.

For CZ, the crypto-to-crypto arrangement offered an obvious advantage: it meant Binance didn't need to touch the conventional banking system, which was a landmine of laws and regulations. CZ also employed another tactic to avoid tangling with the Treasury Department and myriad other agencies in the United States and Europe: He based Binance in small island nations whose governments, eager for business, did not bother much with US-style banking rules. "The strategy in places like the US requires lots of lawyers and lobbyists," CZ says with a grin. "I prefer places like Malta where I can just call up the prime minister and talk to him directly."

CZ's shrewd strategy earned Binance buckets of money. The new exchange was a smash with customers. Those customers, however, still needed a way to convert government-issued money into cryptocurrency in the first place. Many turned to Coinbase. But the San Francisco–based company supported only four cryptocurrencies and levied higher fees than Binance, leading many traders to immediately move their new coins over to CZ's exchange. A refrain began to echo in crypto circles: "Coinbase is just an onramp to Binance." It meant that Coinbase—the longtime star of the crypto scene—had been reduced to the role of a doorman, collecting a cover charge as people poured into a luxury nightclub and ordered bottle service.

For ordinary investors looking to buy a little bit of bitcoin or Ethereum, Coinbase still fit the bill. But to avid traders and hard-core crypto enthusiasts, the lure of Binance Coin and dozens of exotic assets was irresistible. Binance was the future. "We were getting our asses kicked by Binance, and we didn't have a strategy," recalls Coinbase lawyer and political fixer Mike Lempres.

In less than a year, and while Brian and Coinbase were cleaning their shop and waiting for the market to recover, Binance eclipsed Coinbase and other established exchanges to become the most popular crypto service in the world.

● ● ●

Lempres pushed a plan for Coinbase to split into two legal entities—one that did business in heavily regulated places like the United States and another that offered dozens of cryptocurrencies while operating from a regulatory haven like Bermuda. The plan went nowhere, and well into 2018, Coinbase stumbled along with the same four currencies. Longtime engineer Craig Hammell recalls a plan for the company to add Dogecoin, the novelty currency based around the Shiba Inu dog meme in which an adorable pup speaks silly phrases in broken English. Dogecoin had a cult following and would have been easy enough to add in the old days. But with Coinbase's new layers of corporate bureaucracy, it stalled. "We were going to do it," Hammell remembers, "but then it went into all these meetings where someone said they didn't see a return on investment. They didn't get it. Even if it wasn't a money maker, customers wanted more assets and Coinbase wouldn't add them."

The startup where employees had once run through brick walls was now acting more like a stodgy, middle-aged corporation.

Meanwhile, Binance kept cranking out innovations. It debuted a marketing service called Launchpad that invited new crypto projects to buy Binance Coin in exchange for publicity on the exchange. And in a move that underscored CZ's sweeping ambitions, Binance laid plans to challenge Ethereum. Vitalik's smart contract platform was still top dog when it came to hosting other cryptocurrencies—even Binance Coin relied on Ethereum—but CZ concluded it was too slow. The time had come, he decided, for Binance to build its own blockchain.

While Coinbase was dithering over Dogecoin, CZ was laying plans to remake the next era of crypto. His exploits made him a cult figure in the industry. An effusive profile in the trade publication *Coindesk* blared without a hint of irony: "The Unbelievable Brilliance of Binance."

Was CZ as brilliant as all that? Possibly. But some people attribute the rapid rise of Binance at least in part to the hubris of Coinbase and its investors. According to one crypto entrepreneur who has worked in Asian markets, the reason Coinbase didn't see Binance coming is because it's hard to see anything with your head up your ass. "People think crypto is the next trend and therefore Silicon Valley will dominate it," the entrepreneur says. "What's happening here is arrogance and bias in favor of a company that came up in a Western market."

The same clique of investors who made a killing on Facebook and Uber thought Coinbase would create a killer monopoly too. Wrong, says this entrepreneur. The winners in the crypto world will instead be companies like Binance with CEOs who have been battle-tested by Asian markets. "Asia's not in Coinbase's DNA," he says. "I see a cultural gap there that's not closable for them as a company."

Not everyone was awed by Binance. Wences Casares, the early bitcoin visionary from Argentina and CEO of the crypto storage service Xapo, saw Binance as just another crypto cowboy that rose quickly by skirting the rules. Casares predicts CZ will face a fall like Mt. Gox or Poloniex—two other exchanges that once dominated crypto trading but were laid low by scandal and regulatory troubles.

Asiff Hirji, who was charged with battling Binance as Coinbase's COO, also claims the rival exchange is not built to last. Much of the hype around Binance's rise, Hirji suspects, was built on sleazy business practices such as wash trading—a common trick where companies or exchanges take both sides of a trade in order to paint a false picture of user activity. "'Run fast and break things' doesn't work when you're dealing with people's money," says Hirji. "You have to move quickly but you have to aim. What's going to happen is, I think that guy is going to jail. He's a fraud."

People may have disagreed on whether CZ was a genius or a fraud. But in mid-2018, both sides would agree on one point: Binance was indeed kicking Coinbase's ass. By April, Brian and the board finally decided to act. Coinbase needed someone to lead an assault on the bureaucracy enveloping the company. Someone, Brian thought, who could command like a general. What they got was more like a rogue special forces soldier.

15

Power Struggle

Balaji Srinivasan crumbled a Tate's chocolate chip cookie into a bowl, reached for another from the package and crumbled that up, too. Then a third. He took a carton of half-and-half from the fridge, poured it over the crumbs, and began to eat. It was 1:30 in the morning in June of 2018. Balaji looked into the San Francisco night.

Market Street lay enveloped in the uneasy stillness that wraps around a financial district after its daytime energy is drained. The city slept, but Balaji was wide awake. He munched on his bowl of Tate's and half-and-half and thought about crypto.

It had been four years since he had turned up in grubby sweatpants at Coinbase's old Bluxome Street office and expounded on the theories of political economist Albert Hirschman. Employees back then had mistaken him for a hobo at first, but quickly became entranced by his brilliant ideas about money and technology. Now, that brilliance had led Coinbase to hire Balaji as its first chief technology officer.

Balaji was a familiar figure in the Valley. He taught statistics at Stanford and was one of a handful of partners at Andreessen Horowitz, where he was known for PowerPoints that ran over three hundred slides. In 2016, Balaji's expertise on genetics had led the new Trump administration to interview him to run the Food and Drug Administration. As for crypto, Balaji saw it as a subject best left to geniuses. "Blockchains are the most complicated piece of technology to arrive since browsers or operating systems," he declares. "They require a deep understanding of cryptography, game theory, networking, information security, distributed systems, databases, and systems programming. Only a handful of people have that sort of knowledge."

Left unspoken was that Balaji saw himself as one of those people. Coinbase, though, had sought out Balaji for more than his smarts. Since Fred's departure in early 2017, Brian had found it lonely at the top. The arrival of a high-wattage personality like Balaji promised to reintroduce the innovative and hard-driving run-through-walls spirit of the company's early days. "Someone had to play the Fred Ehrsam character. Brian needed the yin to his yang," recalls Nathalie McGrath, who had joined Coinbase in its early days as a chief of staff and rose to VP of People.

Balaji agreed to accept the CTO role, but the price was steep. Getting Balaji meant buying his company, a startup called Earn.com that had begun its life making devices to mine bitcoin but had pivoted to an email introduction service. In Silicon Valley parlance, the deal was an *acqui-hire*—acquiring a company to get the talent who worked there.

Media outlets reported the price of the deal at $120 million, a figure that rankled many of the Coinbase rank and file. "It was a crummy company," claims one Coinbase engineer. "Hiring Balaji was a way for

Andreessen Horowitz to liquidate its dog of a startup." (The VC firm had led Earn.com's Series B funding round.)

Today, board members as well as Coinbase COO Asiff Hirji—himself an Andreessen Horowitz alum—defend the Earn.com acquisition, saying Balaji was worth the cost. More quietly, they add that the real acquisition price was far below the $120 million figure bruited by the media. "You can come up with any sort of deal number you like for public consumption when you factor in hypothetical future payouts. And Balaji has a big ego, so he wanted as big a number as possible," says one Coinbase insider.

. . .

It didn't take long for Balaji and his ego to make an impact at Coinbase. He arrived with a singular mission: help Coinbase compete with Binance by adding new assets.

For months, the company had dithered as Binance grew into a powerhouse by offering dozens of new cryptocurrencies. Meanwhile, Coinbase had plodded along with the same four coins: bitcoin, Ethereum, Litecoin, and—as of late December 2017, after its hiccup of a debut—Bitcoin Cash.

Coinbase's foot-dragging made some sense. The SEC was on the warpath against crypto companies that sold unlicensed securities, and Coinbase—as the self-proclaimed "white knight" of the industry—had to guard its reputation. The company could not become a forum where unscrupulous ICOs peddled shitcoins to Grandma. Still, it was also possible to play it *too* safe—surely, the company could offer more than four tokens.

In addition to playing it safe because of regulators, a big reason Coinbase wasn't offering more than four coins was because its engineering strategy was adrift. Instead of working to support new coins, Coinbase engineers were fiddling with ways to repackage existing offerings—creating bundles and index funds that offered the same boring coins.

In another corner of the office, engineers were at work building something called Toshi. This was a tool to navigate dApps—short for decentralized applications—which Brian and others believed would be the future of crypto. A dApp can be anything from a word-processing tool to a prediction market, but what makes dApps distinct is the lack of a central company or manager. Imagine taking the sort of software programs you find in Microsoft Office and then running them on a bitcoin-style network. Unlike what you find in the app stores of Apple and Google, dApps can be distributed without anyone's permission and rely on random computers around the world to operate. dApps are not the most efficient form of software, not least because you need a special browser to access them in the first place, but their supporters say they represent the next generation of computing.

The future may well revolve around dApps, but in 2018, their outlook looked bleak. Even the most popular dApps had only a few hundred users. Olaf and others questioned why Coinbase was tinkering with Toshi and dApps—especially at a time when millions of people were flocking to Binance to acquire the newest cryptocurrencies. It was as if Coinbase had been a road construction company that instead of laying pavement for interstate highways spent its days adding scenic overlooks or testing new types of gravel. This was a costly mistake, not least because the task of building infrastructure for new coins is intensely technical.

An exchange can offer bitcoin, but that doesn't mean it's easy to offer other cryptocurrencies. Sure, some currencies were created from the same code base as bitcoin or Ethereum—making it easier for an exchange to support them—but they still have their own idiosyncra-sies. Meanwhile, other new currencies had been crafted from a whole new set of code. One of them was Tezos, a new type of blockchain with a built-in voting mechanism that lets owners of Tezos tokens vote for or against proposed upgrades to its software. Adding a currency like Tezos was akin to building a whole new assembly line rather than, as in the case of the bitcoin spin-offs, just modifying an existing line. And in every single case, adding a new currency meant securing more code from omnipresent hackers.

Adding these new currencies was a big job, and Coinbase was playing catch-up. Balaji's arrival was supposed to jump-start the effort, and he didn't disappoint. He had technical chops, and his rep-utation as a crypto visionary inspired the other engineers. He also possessed superhuman stamina. When it was sprint time—Coinbase jargon for bursts of intense work—Balaji would work incessantly for days. He could function without sleep, appearing just as invigo-rated at midnight as at seven in the morning. And he barely slowed down to eat, fueling himself for days at a time with his Tate's and half-and-half.

Even amid Coinbase's workaholic culture, Balaji stood out. Physically, he stood out, too. Typically clad in a hoodie, his intense eyes, spiky hair, bushy eyebrows, and salt-and-pepper stubble make him look like a hungry wolverine. Unfortunately for many at Coin-base, he also *acted* like a wolverine—tearing through anyone who presented an obstacle. "Balaji is not a bad guy. But he's like a cannon-ball, and if you can't explain why you're in his way, God help you—he'll go right through you," says a Coinbase employee.

In short order, Balaji would fulfill the board's hope by shred-ding through much of the bureaucracy that had come to envelop Coinbase. But he would also try to shred many of the people he encountered, including new COO Asiff Hirji, who had lobbied to bring Balaji aboard in the first place.

. . .

Raised in Calgary, a Canadian oil town with a deep conservative streak, Asiff had spent a decade in Silicon Valley before joining Coinbase. But in appearance and outlook, he still comes across as an East Coast banker—a holdover from his stint as a senior executive at TD Ameritrade in New York City. Asiff's fondness for crisp white shirts and expensive blazers made him an odd fit for a West Coast crypto company. It didn't take long for tension to emerge.

"I remember this very, very awkward dinner," says a senior figure at Coinbase, recalling Asiff's arrival in December of 2017. "Asiff introduced himself as chief operating officer and president of the East Coast. The second title hadn't been part of the deal, but Asiff explained to Brian that president is the same thing as COO in the east. It was total BS."

The rest of the table watched the exchange and wondered what the hell was going on. Had this guy come in to help Brian or to replace him?

Asiff's first introduction to the Coinbase rank and file went no better. At a Friday morning all-hands meeting, Asiff ascended a small stage at the front of the room and proceeded to ream out the staff. "I'm embarrassed about our products," he told the assembled engineers in the imperious tone of a corporate executive. He explained he would be tightening things up.

He may have been right, but his approach did not go over well, especially given that he appeared to many as a crypto carpetbagger. For a lot of people in the room, crypto wasn't just a product. It was an idea and a way of life they'd pursued with passion for years. Now they were being berated by some suit who not only had just come to crypto, but who had had the gall to go on TV the week before and speak for Coinbase about its significance. The engineers, especially, seethed. "He saw Coinbase as a lot of egotistical, emotional millennials," recalls Craig Hammell. "We thought, 'Who are you to go on CNBC and act like an expert about all this?'"

As the weeks passed, Asiff would learn other lessons about managing millennials. As someone who had come up in the stern culture of consulting and corporate banking, Asiff faced a steep learning curve. He would deliver a speech only to learn later that employees had complained that his words had triggered them. What the hell did this even mean? he wondered. "Asiff was not used to the idea of people being 'triggered,'" Nathalie recalls.

But even as he fumbled interpersonal relationships, Asiff succeeded in imposing order on the chaos he had found upon arriving at the company. He cleaned up Coinbase's unstable trading systems. He brought in a layer of C-suite executives. And, along with recently added VP of Business, Emilie Choi, he introduced a get-shit-done decision-making process they had learned from East Coast management stalwarts Bain & Company. The process was called RAPID—Recommend, Agree, Perform, Input, Decide—and it was a helpful antidote to Brian who, when called on to make an important decision, had increasingly taken to making no decision at all.

Asiff had been shaped by New York and worked in San Francisco. But it was a third city—Chicago—that preoccupied him at Coinbase. The Windy City and its legions of options and commodities traders were the key to the future of crypto, he believed. "People don't understand this, but the biggest traders of crypto are Chicago's electronic market makers and prop shops. They're the ones who took the crypto marketplace from random tech enthusiasts trading with each other and created a pool of deep liquidity with dependable order books," he says.

"Prop shops" refers to investment firms where partners deploy their own money to profit from trading strategies, while "electronic market makers" specialize in dealing in specific stocks and commodities. While both are fixtures of the New York finance world, their major presence in Chicago testifies to that city's role as an engine of American finance.

In Asiff's view, the crypto engineers of San Francisco may have been brilliant coders, but when it came to market making, they were a bunch of amateurs who might as well have been making food delivery apps. The real talent, the people who knew how to build financial infrastructure, were in Chicago. And that's where Coinbase should go, he declared. He pushed the company to open an office in the city's Loop District off Lake Michigan and staff it with executives and engineers poached from the famed Chicago Mercantile Exchange.

Asiff also oversaw the creation of an over-the-counter desk at Coinbase—a service long offered by competing exchanges like Circle and Gemini—that catered to traders seeking to move large volumes of crypto discreetly. He also insisted Coinbase create a custody service where institutional clients like mutual funds could store crypto assets in compliance with federal regulations.

All of this together was a big bet on a decidedly corporate future for Coinbase. A future that stripped crypto of all idealism, all of its outlaw character. Asiff didn't care one bit about Satoshi's libertarian visions. He believed instead that Coinbase needed to weave its services around the long-established fixtures of Wall Street and Chicago. Better to get a head start hitching the company's wagon to the financial establishment, he argued, than cater to an unpredictable consumer market.

For many in the San Francisco office, Asiff's vision was about as inspiring as a punk rock band that signs an endorsement deal with Brooks Brothers. More seriously, it risked a strategic muddle, given Balaji's quest to challenge Binance by adding exotic cryptocurrencies to Coinbase's platform. It didn't take long for the competing visions—Wall Street versus libertarian utopia—to produce factions at Coinbase, with crypto true believers lining up behind Balaji and the corporate-leaning types backing Asiff.

Conflicting visions in a company are not uncommon. Conflict can even be beneficial as long as there is a CEO who can manage competing factions in the way Abraham Lincoln did with his "Team of Rivals" cabinet. Unfortunately, Coinbase did not have a Lincoln at its head. It had Brian. And Brian, who did not like conflict, could only stand by as the factions threatened to tear each other—and his company—apart.

* * *

"Some people lead by loyalty and inspiration. Balaji leads by fear and by money," says Nathalie McGrath who, as Coinbase's VP of People, watched as infighting engulfed the company.

Balaji's style as he led the charge for a noncorporate vision of crypto was abrasive but effective. For someone who by all accounts did not work well with others, Balaji was remarkably good at office politics. Anyone in his way got edged aside with alacrity. Balaji either fired them outright or, through back-office maneuvering, stripped them of influence until, totally demoralized, they quit on their own accord.

Among these casualties was Adam White. The former Air Force commander and Coinbase employee number five had risen to run the company's professional trading exchange and, in his latest role, was in charge of the company's new office in New York City. But in

Balaji's view, the New York office was supporting the corporate vision of the future and would divert resources from his obsession—adding new cryptocurrency assets—so the office and its staff had to be demeaned and diminished. Adam knew what was up. "Asiff cared about decorum in an office environment and tried to carry himself that way," says Adam. "But Balaji was cutthroat and manipulative. He had this political genius. He would be the ideal person to be on *Survivor*."

Adam was okay with this. He had new opportunities. Wall Street was at last waking up to the potential of cryptocurrency. The New York Stock Exchange came calling, telling Adam in confidence about an ambitious plan to offer bitcoin futures and work on a crypto deal with Starbucks. Would he like to be the new project's COO? Hell yes, he would.

Adam flew back to Coinbase headquarters and broke the news to Brian. Years ago, the early Coinbase crew had instituted something called a "walk and talk"—a way to get out of the office, get some air, and speak frankly. Now, treading the streets of San Francisco, Adam and Brian went for their final walk and talk. For more than ninety minutes, the pair engaged in another Coinbase ritual—candid comments about how the other could improve. Brian offered friendly advice and encouraged Adam to bring their shared spirit of crypto evangelism to the East Coast. For his part, Adam offered a subtle plea for his longtime boss to rein in warring factions at his company. "Brian, at the end of the day, it's you and you alone who can shape the culture of this company as the CEO," he said.

Good advice is not always heeded, and in this case, the politics and power struggles went on unabated as Balaji pushed out designers and a head engineer. Also toppled was Mike Lempres, the veteran legal fixer who had tried to get Brian to warm to Washington, DC. Lempres had worked at the top levels of the Justice Department and once, as a side hustle, he had served as mayor for the affluent Silicon Valley town of Atherton. But none of this compared to what he saw at Coinbase in late 2018. "I've been the mayor of a California town, but I've never seen a place as political as Coinbase," he said on his way out the door in the spring of 2019.

Lempres would remain philosophical about his ouster and still speaks warmly of Brian, if not of his lieutenants. "I would be such an asshole if I was a billionaire at his age," he observes. "And he's not."

Soon after, Coinbase lost Nathalie McGrath, who years before had helped the startup overcome its "Vulcan banker" culture by introducing a spirit of warmth and humanity, had endured bomb threats, and had seen her fill of office warfare. Unlike Lempres, she felt less forgiving. "Balaji was Coinbase's first brilliant jerk," she recalls, "and it changed the culture of our leadership. That's why I left. The heart and soul of what I built is gone."

The departures of longtime fixtures like Adam and Nathalie did not trouble Asiff, who regarded employee churn as ordinary. In Silicon Valley, he says, every startup outgrows its early managers, and the executive team will turn over four or five times if a company is scaling up fast. Besides, amid all the drama, he and Balaji were doing a lot to fix Coinbase's earlier problems.

In April, the company hired a banking veteran, Alesia Haas, as CFO. Finally, there would be someone to reform Coinbase's loosey-goosey cash management system. And the firm's scattershot approach to strategy began to tighten up.

In early 2018, the vice president of Coinbase's Consumer Group, Dan Romero, boasted to *Business Insider* that the company was becoming the "Google of Crypto"—a tagline the public relations team pushed to others in the media. It was a neat phrase. Being the Google of anything sure sounds good. But what did it mean? Google had lots of successful products—YouTube, Gmail, Docs, Cloud, and so on. But Coinbase only had one product anyone cared about. Meanwhile, it was squandering money on experiments that had no obvious appeal, like Toshi.

One benefit of Balaji's wrecking-ball approach was that the secondary projects got sidelined or smothered, and Coinbase moved to focus on his priority—adding new cryptocurrencies. Coinbase unveiled new currency offerings like XRP and Ethereum Classic for US customers, and dozens more for clients overseas. The gap with Binance started to shrink.

But as Balaji consolidated power and sidelined lesser rivals, it became harder to avoid direct collisions with Asiff, who continued to push a strategy centered on Chicago and Wall Street. Tension between the two was palpable at executive meetings. The conflict became so strident that, in time, rumors would swirl in crypto circles that Balaji and Asiff had come to blows. Like many juicy startup rumors, this wasn't true, but screaming matches occurred whenever Asiff pushed the company down a corporate path. "Balaji would jump in and yell, 'Fuck all that! We need to add assets!'" says a former senior Coinbase executive who sat in the meetings.

Realpolitik replaced the idealism Brian had always tried to impart. This became even clearer in early 2019, when the company set out to buy a blockchain analytics service. Coinbase had long relied on a service called Chainalysis, a firm known for creating forensics reports for law enforcement, to provide it with data about blockchain activity. But after Chainalysis insisted on parsing data about Coinbase customer wallets—and after an Israeli security firm reported that a Coinbase account had been funneling bitcoin donations to the terrorist group Hamas—the company dropped Chainalysis in order to bring its analytics service in-house.

Rather than build it, they bought it. In February, Coinbase triumphant-ly announced the acquisition of Neutrino, an Italian analytics startup known for its work analyzing blockchains in Europe. Unfortunately, Neutrino's founders also headed up a company called Hacking Team, which had colluded on spying operations with some of the nastiest gov-ernments around the globe, including the Saudi intelligence unit that orchestrated the murder of *Washington Post* journalist Jamal Khashoggi. Reporters Without Borders had labeled Hacking Team an "enemy of the internet" for spy work it had conducted on behalf of despots in Somalia and Morocco. It was clear that Neutrino's founders were cold-blooded mercenaries. And now they were Coinbase's newest employees.

An uproar ensued as crypto journalist David Z. Morris set out the new hire's ugly past. In response, Coinbase's normally sharp PR team dithered for days, initially brushing off the allegations as uninformed and then claiming the company's higher-ups knew nothing about the Hacking Team's activities. That didn't work. Public outrage grew louder, and a new hashtag began trending on crypto social media: #DeleteCoinbase.

The apparent duplicity of senior management didn't play any bet-ter among Coinbase employees. "They knew about it," says engineer Craig Hammell. "It showed a lack of understanding of what crypto is all about. This is not like other industries. Crypto is driven by the philosophies and ideals behind it."

As the scandal rumbled on, Brian finally acted. After weeks of inertia, he went to where he was most comfortable: writing a blog, where he announced that Coinbase had screwed up and that the com-pany would part ways with anyone who had worked at Hacker Team. "Bitcoin—and crypto more generally—is about the rights of the indi-vidual and about the technological protection of civil liberties," he wrote. "We will fix this and find another way to serve our customers while complying with the law."

But even as Brian tamped down one crisis, another was coming to a head. The battle between Asiff's and Balaji's factions raged on, and Balaji seemed to have the upper hand. By early 2019, many of Asiff's pet projects lay in tatters.

The biggest blow to Asiff came in April 2019, when Coinbase abruptly shut its Chicago office and sent thirty people packing. The move came amid growing opposition to Asiff's corporate vision as Balaji amassed more allies and more power, but it also came down to dollars and cents. Crypto winter had dragged on for so long that even Coinbase began to feel pinched. It didn't help that word leaked to the longtime San Francisco engineers that their Chicago counterparts were making more money than they were. Silicon Valley techies are used to being the top earners—Asiff's decision to pay more for talent in the Midwest came as an affront. Shutting down Chicago solved multiple problems, even if it was a black eye for Asiff.

Balaji was winning the internal political struggle, but he wasn't handling it graciously. In a meeting where Balaji set out his latest road map for adding new crypto assets, Asiff asked a sensible question: Was there a process to *delist* assets? Balaji snapped. "Why are you even asking about this when you don't know anything about crypto?" he sneered at the company's president and COO.

It looked bad for Asiff. In less than a year, Balaji had sown deep divisions in Coinbase, pushed out many longtime employees, thwarted all kinds of projects that didn't benefit his vision, and even got an entire office shuttered. He had also added many new cryptocurrencies—by mid-2019, Coinbase offered dozens of coins in markets around the world—and shook up a tired bureaucracy. And then he quit.

Coinbase's board had structured Balaji's contract to pay him richly once a period of time—in this case, one year—had elapsed, a typical arrangement in the Valley. And like others before him, Balaji waited until the moment those riches rained down, and then, vested, he left to do something else.

Balaji's departure in early May would end the factional drama that had roiled the company. Asiff, suddenly and unexpectedly, saw an opening to have a free hand running Coinbase. He took the bold step of asking Brian in mid-2019 if Brian would report to him, Asiff, on questions of product.

Asiff had overplayed his hand. He had regarded himself as the company's de facto CEO, and for months had acted that part. In the process, he had exhausted much of his political capital at the executive level. Coinbase's true crypto believers had never warmed to him, and still wouldn't even if Balaji was gone. Coinbase's real CEO at last reasserted himself. It was time for Brian to take charge of his company again. He told Asiff, *"No!"*

Asiff took the rejection poorly. Rather than accept a reduced role, he declared he would resign. Brian obliged. And in a moment that still rankles Asiff, he was quickly shown the door without any sort of formal farewell or chance to say goodbye to his staff. The two men haven't spoken since.

Asiff says now that Brian has a lot to learn as a leader: "Brian is a genuinely good person, but he struggles with what his role is. Every successful CEO is one of three things—a product visionary, a culture and talent magnet, or a super salesman. Brian doesn't fit any of those roles."

• • •

Weeks later, Brian sat looking at a ship on the Hudson River, not giving a damn about Asiff or his opinions. He was at TAK, a country club–style restaurant in New York's glitzy new Hudson Yards development, and he felt at ease sitting among friends—real friends.

Adam had joined him for dinner, and so had Fred Ehrsam. Outwardly, Fred bore little resemblance to the hard-charging trader who had slung millions of dollars at Goldman Sachs and then Coinbase. He had become preoccupied with high fashion and taken to wearing tie-dyed fur vests and moonboots. And he no longer spent his evenings glued to a Reddit screen. Now, he ran with Kanye West and other celebrities.

What had not changed was his friendship with Brian. The two were tighter than ever. Now, Fred was eager to talk Brian into exploring his other newfound interests, including fasting, which had become a craze among rich tech executives.

When the talk turned to crypto, Adam and Fred congratulated Brian on taking his company back, and the three reminisced about the exploits that had seen them take Coinbase from a ramshackle apartment into a multibillion-dollar company. They drank and laughed, and for a few precious hours, Brian felt like he had back in the Bluxome Street days when Coinbase was a small startup.

Outside, a heatwave was descending on New York. And crypto winter was beginning to thaw.

16

Bitcoin Triumphant

The depth of crypto winter came on December 15, 2018. On that day, the price of bitcoin dipped to $3,200—more than 80 percent below its high a year earlier. The handful of mainstream media outlets still reporting on crypto noted how far the industry had fallen, and a few pundits pronounced that this time bitcoin was dead for good. Then, as had happened so many times before, bitcoin responded to predictions of its demise by going on a bull run.

The uptick was almost imperceptible at first. In February of 2019, bitcoin shuffled above $4,000, and then, in what would become known as the April Fools' Day rally, the price shot up nearly $1,000 in a single day. By May, bitcoin was trading above $8,000, and in June it hit the $12,000 mark before settling around $10,000 for the rest of the summer. Longtime bitcoin owners smiled in satisfaction while the hedge fund money that had fled rushed back in. The buzz spread to the financial pages. Bitcoin was back.

Not all crypto was back though. The altcoins, aka "shitcoins," born in the ICO boom still stank. The prices of many remained down over 90 percent, and there was no mystery why: all of the grand blockchain projects the ICOs were supposed to fund failed to materialize, and most still consisted of little more than a white paper. Investors had prepaid for tokens on some marvelous ride—only to discover the ride was never going to get built and the tokens were now worthless.

In some cases, the projects failed because the ICO promoters were crooks. But in other cases, the projects didn't launch because the backers found it hard to stay motivated once they were swimming in cash. Good intentions failed as ICO founders discovered it was more agreeable to travel the world and speak at conferences than to labor away over blockchain code.

Even bitcoin's biggest rivals couldn't escape the altcoin wipeout. By July, even as the price of bitcoin had increased 62 percent from a year earlier, Ethereum was *down* 68 percent. It turned out that Ethereum, which had been hailed as a new and better version of bitcoin, had repeated some of bitcoin's mistakes. Long-promised upgrades to its code base never materialized, meaning that the Ethereum blockchain remained slow and inefficient. Meanwhile, the person best poised to lead improvements to Ethereum, Vitalik Buterin, appeared to be getting swallowed by his cult of personality. One of crypto's more memorable memes, "Vitalik Clapping," shows the Ethereum creator on a New York City party boat, pressing his hands together like an alien learning how to applaud. Around him, a gaggle of fresh-faced acolytes look on as a singer serenades him with a bizarre refrain, "Vitalik Clapping, Vitalik Impress. Happy and Clapping, Vitalik Is Impress." Even by the out-there social mores of crypto, it was weird.

Bitcoin's other would-be rival, Bitcoin Cash, had basically collapsed. The currency born in the bitter schism over block size was down

75 percent during the same one-year period bitcoin had gained 62 percent. What's more, it was engulfed in schisms of its own as renegade factions pushed successfully to split the Bitcoin Cash blockchain. Once regarded as a potential replacement for bitcoin, it now looked like an ugly knockoff.

As badly as Ethereum and Bitcoin Cash were faring, they still enjoyed market caps of billions of dollars and a loyal base of fans and developers. The same couldn't be said of the legions of shitcoins tumbling in an unending free fall.

During the height of crypto mania, the phrase "pre-Cambrian explosion" became a staple of conference chatter. It implied the launch of thousands of cryptocurrencies was akin to the myriad life-forms that had sprung up in the early days of evolution on Earth. By 2019, pundits were using a different phrase from the world of biology: "extinction event." The gloomier ones predicted that more than two thousand shitcoins would die off like woolly mammoths.

Longtime bitcoin boosters—at least those who hadn't also invested heavily in altcoins—gloated over this turn of events. They even gave themselves a name—adding yet another term to the ever-growing body of crypto argot. They called themselves "bitcoin maximalists."

. . .

By mid-2019, bitcoin again was the undisputed king of the crypto world. But it wasn't the only bright spot in the industry. Another came in the form of stablecoins, a crypto innovation that would create hundreds of billions of dollars of value and pique the interest of one of the most powerful corporations in the world.

Stablecoins came as a response to one of the most common knocks on bitcoin: extreme volatility. What good was a new type of money if its value fluctuated dramatically every few hours? Stablecoins addressed this problem by providing all the benefits of blockchain-based currency—easy transfers, tamper-proof ledgers, and so on—without that volatility. A bona fide stablecoin would always be worth one US dollar, or fluctuate no more than a penny above or below that. As they grew in popularity, other stablecoins would appear that mirrored the value of other major currencies like the yen or the British pound.

Stablecoins weren't new in 2019. The best known one, called Tether, had appeared in 2015. It caught on with traders who wanted to move in and out of various cryptocurrencies without the fees that came with converting from crypto to traditional currency. Tether, however, suffered from a sketchy reputation. How, traders wondered, could they be sure Tether coins were actually worth a greenback? The shadowy organization that oversaw Tether assured users that there was a reserve to back every single Tether with a dollar—yet they refused to undergo an audit to prove this. This was suspicious. Such suspicions have only mounted in light of Tether's ties to the controversial exchange Bitfinex, and in the wake of a fraud investigation by New York's attorney general.

Tether wasn't the only stablecoin to prompt questions about what was propping it up. In early 2018, a stablecoin startup called Basis raised $133 million from blue-chip investors like Bain Capital and Google Ventures. Basis proposed to keep its coin stable by issuing bonds every time it fell below $1. The plan didn't make much sense, given there was no guarantee people would buy the bonds. Meanwhile, the SEC warned that the bond plan amounted to selling securities. Basis gave up in short order and returned most of the money it had raised.

What did make sense, when it came to stablecoins, was to peg their value to a reserve of US dollars and conduct third-party audits to prove the dollars were really there. This is what Coinbase did in the summer of 2019, working with rival Circle to create a new cryptocurrency called USD Coin. Meanwhile, the Winklevoss twins created a stablecoin of their own called Gemini Dollar. Soon these and a growing array of other stablecoins provided credibility to the concept and challenged Tether as fixtures of crypto trading markets. By 2020, Coinbase and others were paying interest on customers' stash of stablecoins—a sign of how cryptocurrency could resemble an ordinary savings account.

More importantly, the growth of stablecoins signaled to important people outside the crypto world that blockchain-based money could transform finance. National governments, which had long looked at crypto with suspicion, began to experiment with stablecoins as a way to issue money. Then, in June of 2019, Facebook dropped a bombshell.

Rumors had swirled for months that the social network was going to launch a cryptocurrency, but the company's plans, dubbed Project Libra, turned out to be bigger and more ambitious than many had imagined. Libra, its new currency, would be pegged to a basket of global currencies—including dollars, euros, and Swiss francs—and available to Facebook users around the world. This meant that anyone who used Facebook, or one of the company's other products like Instagram or WhatsApp, would have easy access to the new currency.

Even more remarkable was that Facebook had assembled a coalition of A-list brands in finance and technology as partners, including Visa, Mastercard, Uber, Spotify, and eBay. Facebook's master plan called for its partners to help maintain dozens of blockchain nodes that would create a transaction ledger for Libra, and to contribute to the reserve fund that would back the Libra with hard currency.

The partner list included two companies that specialized in storing cryptocurrency, and it also included Coinbase. There already was a link between Facebook and Coinbase: the head of Project Libra was David Marcus, a former president of PayPal who, until recently, had been on Coinbase's board of directors. But while Silicon Valley gossips have speculated for years that Facebook has tried to acquire Coinbase, the rumors are false—Facebook never even inquired, and Brian Armstrong and Mark Zuckerberg have never met.

When it came to Project Libra, the plan was for Coinbase to be just one of a hundred or so partners to help Facebook run the new blockchain network—if it ever got off the ground in the first place. Unfortunately for Facebook, by the time it announced Libra, the company had become radioactive to Congress and regulators around the world. The social network was already the subject of numerous antitrust investigations, and for many governments, the prospect of Facebook controlling a global supply of money was beyond the pale. Meanwhile, some of Facebook's high-profile partners, including Visa and PayPal, became skittish of the political heat and bolted the consortium.

The Libra plan wasn't just a political minefield—some feared it was also an economic one. Katharina Pistor, a professor at Columbia Law School, told *Fortune* magazine that Libra could destabilize the exchange rate in developing economies like Kenya if currency traders used Facebook's money instead of the local currency. Others likened Libra to a gambit by a handful of companies to privatize the money supply. A few suggested it was tantamount to outright treason. "If Facebook raised an army, this would be only slightly more hostile to the people of the United States than what is currently proposed," declared Preston Byrne, an outspoken cryptocurrency lawyer.

Critics raised many valid questions, and, as of the time of this writing, it's far from clear whether Facebook can overcome government opposition and actually launch Project Libra. What is clear is that Silicon Valley is still able to dream up grand and world-changing technologies—whether or not the rest of the world wants to embrace them. It also shows that those technologies are likely to disrupt global finance.

If the US government won't allow crypto to blossom, it's very likely China will. The People's Republic has already tasked its central bank with creating a digital version of its currency, the renminbi. For the Communist Party, the advantages are twofold: digital currency can be used to surveil Chinese citizens more closely than ever, and it will be a tool to pressure other countries to abandon the US dollar as the world's main reserve currency. If this begins to take place, it's a safe bet Congress and the United States will look at Facebook's Libra in a different light.

. . .

Governments may have greeted Facebook's digital currency plans with surprise and alarm, but in crypto circles, Project Libra mostly generated guffaws. This wasn't real cryptocurrency but a debased version, one that would be controlled by a cabal of powerful companies. Veteran crypto boosters invoked the c-word—*centralized*—and warned people to avoid it.

Suspicions of the new corporate cryptocurrency, coupled with the ongoing slump of altcoins, led bitcoin's halo to shine brighter than ever. Satoshi's currency was now a decade old and more secure than ever. To underscore the point, crypto billionaire and early Coinbase investor Barry Silbert launched a wave of national TV commercials urging investors to drop gold and buy bitcoin. Meanwhile, the venerable brokerage firm Charles Schwab published a list in late 2019 of the most commonly held stocks by the millennial generation. The list was topped by Amazon, Apple, Tesla, and Facebook. Number five, ahead of Berkshire Hathaway and Disney, was a stock called Grayscale Bitcoin Trust that offers a way for investors to buy bitcoin in the form of a share.

Bitcoin's resilience—the network has run without interruption for over ten years—resulted in yet more memes. "The Fed Wire is Down. Bitcoin is never down," tweeted a crypto fund manager and social media personality known as Pomp. He followed this with: "The stock market is closed. Bitcoin never closes." Hundreds of other crypto disciples chimed in with their own aphorisms—"Banks close your account without notice. Bitcoin never closes your account." And so on.

The buzz around bitcoin in mid-2019 felt like a religious revival. The oldest cryptocurrency had triumphed over rival sects that had sprung up around different altcoins, and bitcoin believers felt their god was on top once and for all. That didn't mean bitcoin didn't have powerful enemies—including the president of the United States.

"I am not a fan of bitcoin and other Cryptocurrencies, which are not money, and whose value is highly volatile and based on thin air," huffed President Trump in a Twitter tirade, adding that crypto had been tied to unlawful behavior. The July outburst appeared tied to news about Facebook's Project Libra and to Trump's general hostility to the tech industry.

The presidential outburst produced a backlash, ironically, among fringe alt-right figures who were normally staunch Trump supporters. Meanwhile, ordinary bitcoin enthusiasts celebrated that the president's outburst caused only a small dip in the currency's price. To them, it was yet more evidence of bitcoin's resilience.

For Brian and others at Coinbase, bitcoin's 2019 resurgence felt like the return of an old friend—not least because the company's revenues began surging anew on the higher price and an upswing of trading volume. And inside the company, ordinary employees cheered the return of Brian to day-to-day decision making. Asiff's presence had been, for many, never natural or right—only a crypto believer like Brian could lead a company like Coinbase. He had also found in Emilie Choi, the LinkedIn veteran he promoted to succeed Asiff as COO, a trusted lieutenant who could quell internal political battles.

On the business front, the company was still lagging behind Binance, but the gap between the two was shrinking, in part because Coinbase now offered dozens of cryptocurrencies in markets around the world. Meanwhile, Binance's star lost some of its luster after the exchange suffered a major hack that saw thieves plunder $40 million worth of bitcoin. At the same time, CZ's run-and-gun style with regulators had become more perilous as rumors swirled about looming investigations by the SEC and other agencies.

Meanwhile, Coinbase's latest attempt to diversify its income away from trading commissions showed signs of success. Since early 2018, Coinbase had been building out a service called Custody, which allowed funds and wealthy individuals to store their crypto for a small fee. The Custody service also opened the door to offer other crypto-based financial services such as lending and proxy voting for block-chains like Tezos. And in a nod to how crypto trading was becoming ever more like traditional finance, Coinbase outbid Binance to acquire a prime brokerage called Tagomi, which had been founded by a senior Goldman Sachs executive.

In doing all this, Coinbase and its rivals were adding layers of infra-structure that had existed in the traditional banking industry for years. Maybe Asiff wasn't all wrong. Wall Street and Silicon Valley were growing closer together—a point underscored when Coinbase beat out Fidelity, the epitome of old-school East Coast investment firms, in a bid to acquire bitcoin storage business Xapo. Coinbase's $55 million acquisition also saw the company take possession of nearly eight hundred thousand new bitcoins. By the end of summer 2019, Coinbase would control more than 5 percent of all bitcoins in existence.

17

The Future of Finance

The JP Morgan Chase Tower stretches fifty-two stories above Manhattan's fabled Park Avenue, an imposing glass declaration of power and prestige. From one perch on the forty-ninth floor are stunning views of Central Park and midtown, along with fine art and a glass case that displays the pistols used by Vice President Aaron Burr to kill the country's first treasury secretary, Alexander Hamilton, in a duel. There's a bar and a long table where bankers and their guests dine high above the city. Presiding over all of it is Jamie Dimon, the most influential banking CEO in the world and bitcoin's most famous, most powerful nemesis.

Dimon has thick white-gray hair, soft features, and piercing blue eyes. One spring morning in 2019, he rose and trained those eyes on a CEO half his age who'd arrived from California. He extended his hand, and Brian shook it. The two men turned and stared out the windows of Dimon's office at the financial capital of the world.

For Brian, the clandestine meeting was an opportunity to learn. Still possessed of his insatiable desire for self-improvement, Brian asked Dimon for insights about the financial system. He had recently done the same with Lloyd Blankfein, the senior chairman of Goldman Sachs.

Dimon's motives for the meeting were less obvious. Beyond the good grace of mentoring a younger executive, why would crypto's most prominent critic sit down with one of its biggest advocates? As it turned out, Dimon's views of crypto were a lot more nuanced than media caricatures would imply. And part of him was simply tired of being asked about it.

Later, people would come to understand this. "I didn't want to be the spokesman against bitcoin. I don't really give a shit—that's the point, OK?" Dimon said in an interview.

What Dimon said about crypto was surprising. More surprising still was what he had *done* about crypto. Over five years, while he had publicly ranted against about bitcoin and dismissed crypto, he had also quietly encouraged ambitious blockchain research inside JP Morgan. This included the creation of Quorum, a spin-off of Ethereum that serves as a private network and ledger for financial transactions. He had even approved JPM Coin, a new cryptocurrency to settle cross-border payments with clients.

At the same time JP Morgan was dabbling with crypto, Coinbase was moving closer to traditional banking. The one-time startup was applying for a federal bank charter, a powerful license that would open the door to offering FDIC-insured deposits and give Coinbase direct access to the Federal Reserve. Without realizing it, the two leaders, seemingly as far apart ideologically as their offices were geographically, had been moving toward each other.

By 2019, the worlds of Wall Street and Silicon Valley were suddenly not so far apart. Coinbase had spent the year playing catch up to

Binance. But, "in the long term, it's not Coinbase versus Binance," says Barry Silbert, the early Coinbase investor and bitcoin billionaire. "It's Coinbase versus JP Morgan."

Silbert's prediction may come true in the long term, but in 2020 the upstart Coinbase and the senior incumbent of finance, JP Morgan, would come together in a surprising way. Brian and Dimon's meeting, it turned out, had laid the groundwork for JP Morgan to take Coinbase on as a banking customer. Only five years earlier, startup-friendly Silicon Valley Bank had cut off Coinbase over fears about bitcoin, and now the most venerable financial firm on Wall Street had agreed to handle its money.

• • •

It's an axiom that we overestimate the impact of technology in the short term and underestimate it in the long term. That's certainly true of the consumer internet, whose arrival in the 1990s produced a frenzy of speculation and then a spectacular crash. Barry Schuler, who was CEO of one of the dot-com boom's most famous companies, America Online, recalls what happened next: "When the cool-down came, a lot of the media establishment breathed easy and said, 'We don't have to worry about that.' AOL's market collapsed and everyone was like, 'Thank God that was a fad.' Now, of course, Netflix is killing media companies."

As a longtime member of Coinbase's board, Schuler sees the same phenomenon taking hold. The Wall Street establishment, he says, has become smugly complacent about crypto since the collapse of the 2017 bubble. But Schuler says the status quo can't last. "Look back at the first phase of the internet from the '90s to now," he continues, "and look at all the businesses that have been disrupted—from retail to media to advertising. Financial services is basically untouched. They've built a transaction layer on top of their core services so people can check their accounts but everything underneath is archaic and obsolete. And this is the largest industry in the world."

Schuler predicts that Wall Street is on the cusp of the same massive internet-driven disruption that befell so many other industries. Blockchain, he says, will give rise to a new token-based financial system that will radically transform traditional debt and equity markets.

The question is whether banks and old-school financial firms will adapt to this changing world quickly enough. Alex Tapscott, a CFA and coauthor of the book *Blockchain Revolution*, notes how industry incumbents are rarely at the forefront of technological change.

"Typically, the leaders of old paradigms don't embrace new ones. That's the reason Marriott didn't embrace Airbnb and why the White Pages got replaced by Google," Tapscott says. His observation is a perfect example of "the gale of creative destruction," a phrase coined by legendary economist Joseph Schumpeter, who nearly eighty years ago defined it as "a process of industrial mutation that incessantly revolutionizes the economic structure from within, incessantly destroying the old one, incessantly creating a new one."

But in the case of banks, Tapscott notes, some are more poised to adapt to the impending gale than typical incumbents. He points to JP Morgan's pursuit of blockchain research and to Fidelity, the investment giant with nearly $7 trillion in assets under management that's expanding aggressively into crypto.

Schuler and Tapscott aren't the only ones who believe massive, blockchain-based disruption is coming to Wall Street. Anyone very familiar with crypto is quick to make the case that the technology is so superior to the current system that its adoption is inevitable. They point to the power of digital tokens, which can be used not just as a currency but as a system of tracking ownership and for tamper-proof record keeping. One obvious use for tokens, says Balaji Srinivasan, is for cap tables—the documents that show who owns how many shares in a company, a fixture of the startup and venture capital worlds.

"Right now, cap tables are hand-edited in Excel. With blockchain, all tokens will update automatically. Portfolio management and updating private stock records will become so much easier. There will be no need to nag fifty people to respond to an email," says Balaji, who, after his controversial reign at Coinbase, joined another crypto startup.

Cap tables, though, are just one small piece of the financial world that could be transformed by widespread token adoption. Professor Emin Gün Sirer, a computer scientist and blockchain authority at Cornell University, predicts whole swaths of Wall Street middlemen—notably lawyers and auditors—will be replaced. "The nature of tokens is they lend themselves to easy public scrutiny and auditing," he says. "The technology can't be interfered with, so we won't need many of these middlemen."

Sirer also predicts that every stock certificate will eventually be a token on a blockchain. Once he thought that stock exchanges would drive this change by replacing their shares with tokens. But now he thinks the move to tokens will come when startups decide to raise money on crypto exchanges, turning to companies like Coinbase rather than traditional exchanges. Eventually, Sirer expects the likes of the New York Stock Exchange will buy their crypto counterparts and incorporate them into their existing services.

Sirer has another observation about the future of the crypto industry: As long as the industry is driven by speculation, he says, it will be exchanges—Coinbase, Binance, Kraken, and Gemini—that occupy the most prominent place in crypto. But as the industry matures and tokens become part of the financial mainstream, it could be companies that offer other services—loans, investment advice, or consulting— that become its face.

If Sirer is right, what does this mean for Coinbase? The company has long tried to become more than a trading floor and is gaining traction with new services including its custody business. If it acquires a federal banking charter, Coinbase could evolve into a full-fledged financial services giant.

For now, though, Coinbase's biggest achievement has been closing divisions between ideological bitcoin believers and ordinary consumers. Brian's early insight that everyday people would buy crypto if you offered an easy way to do it proved to be correct. Wences Casares, an early bitcoin entrepreneur and one of the first to introduce crypto to Silicon Valley, sees Coinbase as a pillar of the larger crypto economy. "I think sometimes bitcoin fundamentalists are a bit naïve or simplistic in not realizing that they wouldn't enjoy the high price of bitcoin if Coinbase hadn't created a big market for it," he says.

None of this, though, means Coinbase is destined to be the JP Morgan in a coming era of crypto. A big reason is because, even though everyone familiar with crypto predicts it will disrupt Wall Street, no one's quite sure when.

• • •

"We're in the Apple II phase of crypto. What we really need is the PC," says Chris Dixon, the venture capitalist and Coinbase board member.

Dixon's analogy is a good one. The desktop device Apple launched in 1977 was a hit, but only a small fraction of Americans would ever own one. It would only be four years later with the arrival of the IBM PC that personal computers became mainstream to the point that *Time* magazine declared 1982 the "year of the computer."

Asiff Hirji also thinks something big is coming to crypto but isn't sure when. Despite his awkward exit from Coinbase, his ardor for blockchain technology has only grown. "I view crypto as a third big evolution in tech," he says. "We went from the mainframe to mobile cloud computing, and the next tech phase will be decentralized blockchain computing."

While it's easy to imagine the future of finance as a showdown between the likes of Coinbase and JP Morgan, they're not the only contenders. Tapscott, the *Blockchain Revolution* author, says big tech giants—not just Facebook but Amazon and Apple too—could just as easily dominate crypto. Then there are national governments. Authoritarian regimes like China or Venezuela, Tapscott points out, are developing cryptocurrencies. Their strategic goals involve not only undermining the US dollar's role as the world's reserve currency but using crypto to surveil and control their citizens. "There's a lot of forces coming together in crypto—tech companies, banks, upstart financial companies, and authoritarian governments. It's going to be a heck of a fight," says Tapscott.

Ironically, it's possible that the winner of this fight will be none of these players. Instead, the prevailing force in crypto could be an emerging technology called DeFi—short for decentralized finance. In a DeFi world, bitcoin-like networks would offer financial services like loans or deposits run by smart contracts, all beyond the control of a company or government. DeFi isn't just an idea—a number of projects are already up and running, and CZ, the cowboy CEO of Binance, has launched a decentralized exchange. There are even rumors that CZ plans to move his entire crypto empire to DeFi networks and oversee it from a yacht in international waters, beyond the reach of any regulator.

If this renegade vision of crypto comes to pass, a big reason for it may be the US government's aggressive and incoherent attempt at regulation. In the course of researching this book, interview subjects over and over again shared fears the United States will smother crypto innovation and force it offshore. In the absence of a national crypto policy and laws to support it—similar to the legislation Congress passed in the 1990s to support internet innovation—America runs a very real risk of forfeiting the lead on a world-changing technology.

Sirer believes DeFi has a real chance to be the future of crypto, but he cautions it will be five years until the technology is viable. He also notes that the crypto community's plans to improve existing networks—notably bitcoin and Ethereum—may be out of reach. "Bitcoin relies on narrative tricks. The solution to scaling the network is always 18 months always. It's like Godot. He never arrives," says Sirer, invoking Samuel Beckett's famous existential play.

Sirer isn't the only one to point out how the crypto movement is driven as much by mythology as it is by technology. The Nobel Prize–winning economist Robert Shiller's latest book, *Narrative Economics*, devotes its first chapter to bitcoin. The cryptocurrency, Shiller says, has no intrinsic value but has been propped up by a contagious belief that it does.

Academics like Shiller who are deeply skeptical of crypto, however, belong to a shrinking minority. In recent years, there's been an explosion of crypto and blockchain research on campuses in the United States and around the world. It was only in 2016 that Katie Haun, the former prosecutor and Coinbase board member, began teaching one of the only crypto classes in the country at Stanford. By 2019, 56 percent of the world's top fifty universities offered at least one such class, and some schools now offer many: Cornell's curriculum includes fourteen blockchain-related courses, while Columbia, NYU, and MIT offer at least half a dozen. Also striking is that these classes aren't confined to computer science. Instead, departments as diverse as law, management, humanities, and engineering are teaching crypto courses too.

All of this represents not just a proliferation of knowledge, but a signal that a young generation is aspiring to careers in crypto. Their presence is likely to bring new breakthroughs that solve the scaling problems that have always plagued the blockchain. Meanwhile, some of these students will start companies that will bring new types of crypto and blockchain technology to the financial sector or make crypto accessible to consumers in ways we can't imagine.

. . .

By 2019, Coinbase's security detail began insisting that Brian use aliases even to book a table for a casual drink. So now at restaurants in the Bay Area, the reservation is under Simon Bradshaw, or one of several other British-sounding pseudonyms. It's a small price to pay for running a billion-dollar company.

"Simon" arrives at the nondescript hotel restaurant in San Francisco's financial district wearing his trademark black T-shirt. He orders a soda water. It's all he will have for the evening—a nod to the twenty-four-hour fast Fred has convinced him to try. Brian is polite to the restaurant staff and has shed the "Don't fucking bother me" demeanor he had adopted when Coinbase launched.

I ask him about the future of Coinbase and if there's anything keeping him up at night. Brian's biggest worry, it turns out, is not JP Morgan or Binance or even the long shadow that America's regulators are casting over the crypto industry. It's something he has yet to encounter.

"When Coinbase was in an awkward teenage state, the industry didn't stop. A Generation 2 of crypto came along and started to eat our lunch. Now, there's going to be a Generation 3 crypto company that will be well funded, compliant, and the biggest threat yet," Brian says.

It's a common fear among Silicon Valley entrepreneurs. It's also a very healthy one, given a ceaseless pace of disruption that topples even the most famous companies if they stop innovating.

"I don't want to be become Wall Street or Wells Fargo. I want Coinbase to bring about economic freedom," says Brian. "One of the hardest things to do in business is repeated innovation. The hardest of all is to build a company that survives the test of time." Part of this will necessitate Coinbase one day becoming a public company. Brian demurs when asked when or how this will happen, but people long familiar with Coinbase predict this will entail some combination of a token offering and a traditional IPO.

"It would be pretty boring, wouldn't it?" says cofounder Fred Ehrsam of a conventional listing, adding that Coinbase is "spiritually" built to go public using a blockchain. When it does, it will be another first in Coinbase's long and important legacy of crypto innovation.

Many of Coinbase's former employees are in the process of building crypto legacies of their own. Fred and Olaf are running crypto funds worth hundreds of millions of dollars. Craig Hammell, Coinbase's soft-spoken fourth employee, is planning a startup of his own. He's not sure of the details but likes the idea of working with shopkeepers in South America where more and more local people are turning to bitcoin as a means of shielding their wealth from the disastrous economic policies of their governments.

A common thread among all of their visions is applying Silicon Valley's do-the-impossible attitude to the staid world of finance. "I wish more people would try big ideas and new things," Brian says pensively. "In the early days, I remember when a lot of people described bitcoin as a scam and hung up the phone on us. A lot of people are just scared of new ideas. But one of the things about Silicon Valley is that people are not as skeptical as everywhere else. You can still throw out a crazy idea, and people will get excited."

Epilogue

On March 9, 2020, the Dow Jones Industrial Average dropped a record 2,000 points amid fears over oil prices and the Covid-19 pandemic that had begun to consume the world. Three days later, the Dow fell another 2,350 points, and the following Monday it lost 3,000 more. It was a once-in-a-century financial calamity, and nothing in the market was spared—stocks, bonds, commodities, and even precious metals suffered a dizzying plunge.

So did bitcoin.

Its price dipped below $5,000 on March 16. Only weeks before, the currency had sat above $10,300. Crypto haters gleefully pointed out that, far from being a superior form of gold—something traditionally coveted to protect against financial shocks—bitcoin had choked in this critical moment.

Then, as it did so many times before, bitcoin came roaring back. By June, the price topped $10,000 again, and the original cryptocurrency was posting a better 2020 performance than gold and nearly every other asset. For those who had owned it for years, the episode was yet more proof that bitcoin was the honey badger—able to take any beating and emerge even stronger. Coinbase, meanwhile, rode the volatility to trading riches on the scale of what it enjoyed during the peak of the 2017 bubble.

. . .

In San Francisco, Coinbase's founder waited out the pandemic in his penthouse in the city's tallest building, where his neighbors included NBA star Kevin Durant and other members of the Golden State Warriors. Brian had grasped the implications of the Covid-19 crisis early, and Coinbase's work-from-home blueprint had been shared widely among companies in the Valley and beyond.

But he was hardly the first from the crypto world to warn about what was coming as coronavirus emerged—that designation belonged to Balaji Srinivasan, Coinbase's former CTO who had almost burned the company to the ground in order to save it.

Months before the virus hit the United States with full force, Balaji had been tweeting like a maniac about the disease spreading out of Wuhan, China. His campaign led a tech journalist to mock him as "bubble boy" and, upon being vindicated, Balaji did not respond with quiet satisfaction. Instead, he embarked upon a ruthless grudge match against the media and egged on others to do the same—underscoring how the crypto world, and the Valley at large, has a knack for fostering people with wealth, brilliance, and incredibly thin skin.

The broader crypto community responded to the economic fallout from the disease with—what else—memes. Twitter handles, websites, and other corners of crypto land all adopted a version of the moniker "Fed go brrr," a snarky nod to the US Treasury's mass money printing during the crisis. Many showed the slogan alongside of a bureaucrat cranking out dollars from a printing press.

· · ·

By 2020, the early team that had helped Brian built Coinbase had long since scattered to other ventures, but nearly all remained immersed in crypto. This included the company's second employee, Craig Hammell, who took up a deep study of bitcoin's code as part of a plan to use crypto to help impoverished communities. Employee number three, Charlie Lee, had given himself over to creating new privacy features for Litecoin, the bitcoin rival he had created a decade before.

Olaf Carlson-Wee, who had arrived to join Coinbase with lumberjack sap on his clothes and only a friend's couch to sleep on, had transformed from jester to king. His crypto hedge fund, Polychain Capital, had moved from improvised, ramshackle offices in San Francisco's Mission District to a palatial suite of offices on the city's waterfront. It's hard to avoid such trappings when you control more than a billion dollars of investor funds. But Olaf refused to renounce his eccentricities entirely, dedicating nooks of his corporate palace to his literary hero, David Foster Wallace.

Olaf was not the only early Coinbase vet to undergo a transformation. Adam White was the earnest Californian who had tried to sell old-money powerhouse Cantor Fitzgerald on bitcoin in early 2017, only to be laughed out of the room by a phalanx of Wall Street guys. Three years later, he was a Wall Street guy himself. As president of Bakkt, the New York Stock Exchange's crypto venture, he had become one of the most prominent faces of bitcoin in the traditional finance world. In doing so, he and Coinbase had helped bridge what was once a grand canyon between Silicon Valley and the East Coast financial establishment.

Coinbase alumni were not only spreading the crypto gospel to Wall Street, but to Washington, DC, as well. The company's chief legal officer, Brian Brooks, would come to lead the Office of the Comptroller of the Currency, which oversees the country's banking laws. Meanwhile, two other Coinbase lawyers, Dorothy Dewitt and Andrew Ridenour, would take roles at the CFTC, the nation's powerful commodities regulator.

Their arrivals coincided with a growing realization among some regulators and members of Congress that crypto was not simply a front for crime and chaos, but a powerful technology that could transform money. Slowly, the federal government's antipathy to bitcoin is lifting. Meanwhile, some states are working to welcome it. These include Wyoming, which has passed a series of banking laws that encourage crypto companies to set up shop.

$$\bullet \quad \bullet \quad \bullet$$

All this doesn't mean crypto has lost its outlaw side, of course. A report revealed that scammers took in a record $4 billion in 2019 as a result of crypto hustles, most notably through Ponzi schemes. On social media, the scams became so bad that crypto firm Ripple filed a lawsuit against YouTube over a series of send-us-your-money videos that hijacked the image of its CEO Brad Garlinghouse. Meanwhile, teenagers would hack into Twitter in July of 2020, hijacking the accounts of everyone from Brian to Elon Musk to Michelle Obama in order to invite their millions of followers to send bitcoin. And, in the fifth season of *Billions*, the Showtime series beloved by finance junkies, a key plot point turns on an illegal bitcoin mining operation run by the main character's teenage son.

Overall, though, bitcoin's reputation is better than it's ever been. This is reflected in the mainstream news media, which for a long time ignored crypto stories unless they involved something criminal or salacious. Today, a typical headline is more likely to focus on news like the VC fund Andreessen Horowitz's new $200 million crypto fund, which was launched in April 2020 and is overseen by former prosecutor turned Coinbase board member, Katie Haun.

And while Wall Street and Silicon Valley continue to move to meet each other in the middle with cryptocurrency, some of the old rivalries still flare up. As late as May of 2020, slides from a Goldman Sachs presentation to investors sneered at bitcoin, comparing it to the tulip bulb mania and pointing to its use by criminals. Crypto Twitter shot back immediately, pointing to examples of Goldman's sketchy business dealings and reminding the bank of its abortive attempt to set up a crypto desk of its own, staffed by a pair of young executives with ill-advised man-buns.

Battles between bitcoin believers and analysts at firms like Goldman Sachs are likely to be a permanent part of crypto culture, it seems. That culture, lively as it is, also continues to suffer from an ongoing inability to bring women into its fold. Nathalie McGrath, Coinbase's early head of people who founded a boutique firm dedicated to helping startups with corporate culture, observes that crypto needs "more diversity and representation to truly thrive"—a challenge that is likely to become more pressing as inclusion and social justice issues move to the forefront of US society.

. . .

Making predictions about crypto can be hard, especially since those who do are so often wrong. Many people have wrongly predicted bitcoin's demise, while a good number of others have made equally off-the-mark assurances about the digital currency hitting $100,000 before long.

But one of the better predictions comes from Coinbase cofounder Fred Ehrsam. By 2020, Fred has lost most of his hard-charging "run through brick walls" demeanor, while taking up activities like vipassana, a silent meditation technique. He describes one ten-day retreat that obliged him to reflect without talking, paper, or possessions. The process led him to ruminate about life and ideas that would change the world, and most particularly about crypto.

"The hardest part about getting a new network effects-based technology is the start, and crypto seems to have overcome that initial inertia," says Fred. "The next twenty years, much like the internet, is likely to awe us in ways no one can predict."

Index

Acknowledgments

Bitcoin is a digital currency, but also a technology—one that can be intimidating and difficult to understand at first. Fortunately, there are many people who are passionate to explain the novel aspects of bitcoin and other cryptocurrencies. I met such people the first time I encountered bitcoin at an open air festival in New York City in 2013 and, since then, I've been fortunate to speak with many others who have taken the time to help me understand the splendid technology called blockchain.

Despite its well-deserved reputation for drama and infighting, the cryptocurrency community is also incredibly supportive, and I want to thank those who offered me advice and encouragement during the writing of this book: Laura Shin, Alex Tapscott, Ryan Selkis, Frank Chaparro, Pete Rizzo, Dan Roberts, and Kathleen Breitman.

I'm also grateful to the many current and former employees of Coinbase who took the time to speak candidly with me about the company and share many of its secrets, and to Coinbase's communications team for arranging many interviews. Likewise, I want to thank Barry Silbert, Chris Dixon, Emin Gün Sirer, and the numerous other cryptocurrency theorists and entrepreneurs who helped supply the larger ideas that inform this book.

I could not have written *Kings of Crypto* without the support of my employer, *Fortune* magazine, which not only provided me time to write but also gave me free rein to report and write about cryptocurrency, even when the topics roamed far beyond those familiar to the publication's regular business audience. My appreciation extends in particular to *Fortune* CEO Alan Murray and stellar editors Cliff Leaf, Andrew Nusca, Adam Lashinsky, and Matt Heimer. I'm equally grateful to my fellow writers at *Fortune*, delightful people who have been a frequent source of inspiration and collaboration—especially Jen Wieczner and David Z. Morris.

I owe a debt of gratitude to the Eastham Public Library on Cape Cod, Massachusetts, whose pleasant staff and delightful ambience helped *Kings of Crypto* come into existence. I have also been fortunate for the crack talent and professionalism of Anne Starr and the entire production team at Harvard Business Review Press.

Thanks also to my family, who provided both support and pleasant distraction during the many times when this project consumed nights and weekends, and to my friend Justin Doom for reading early drafts.

Finally, I want to acknowledge three people to whom I'm particularly indebted: my editor at the Press, Scott Berinato, who improved the text at every turn; my agent, Lisa DiMona, who provided energy and encouragement during critical moments in the publication process; and Robert Hackett, my friend and *Fortune* colleague, who not only read the draft but also shares my passion for cryptocurrency and new ideas.

About the Author

Jeff John Roberts is a senior writer and prize-winning reporter at *Fortune* magazine, where he covers cryptocurrency, law, finance, and technology. He has also written for the *New York Times*, *Reuters*, the *Economist*, the *Globe & Mail*, and numerous other mainstream publications, as well as for the *McGill Law Journal*. He is a regular guest on radio and TV news programs, appearing on outlets such as the BBC, NPR, CBC, Fox Business, and CNBC.

A lawyer by training, Roberts passed the bar in both New York State and Ontario, Canada. He became a full-time journalist in 2010 after completing a Master of Arts at Columbia Journalism School. In 2016, he obtained a Master of Science and credits for the first year of an MBA while attending the Knight-Bagehot Fellowship at the Business and Journalism Schools at Columbia. In addition, Roberts holds a BA and an LLB/BCL from the McGill Faculty of Law.

In the course of his journalism career, Roberts has covered the intersection of law and technology, focusing on topics as diverse as high-tech patent litigation, the Federal Communications Commission, and digital payment systems. He has covered blockchain and cryptocurrency since 2013 and regularly interviews the most influential people in the industry.